Come on David!

YOU wouldn't think to look at him now that there was a time when they almost gave him up. Like so many babies he couldn't digest his food. Then someone suggested Nestlé's Milk and from the first feed he came on famously.

Nestlé's Milk is rich, full cream country milk. Nature's own perfect food, specially prepared to make it digestible by the most delicate baby.

RICHEST IN CREAM **Nestlé's Milk**

Fifty years of health and safety
advertising and publicity

HERE'S TO YOUR HEALTH

RUTH ARTMONSKY
& STELLA HARPLEY

For Stella, Becky and Sally,
whose very existence keeps me going.

Published by Artmonsky Arts
Flat 1, 27 Henrietta Street
London WC2E 8NA
www.ruthartmonsky.com
ruthartmonsky@yahoo.co.uk
Tel. 020 7240 8774

Text © Ruth Artmonsky 2014

ISBN 978-0-9573875-8-4

Designed by:
David Preston Studio
www.davidprestonstudio.com

Printed in England by:
Northend Creative Print Solutions,
Clyde Road, Heeley, Sheffield, S8 0TZ

CONTENTS

To Keep Happy,
Keep Well

—a new way of living

INTRODUCTION

The period covered by this book, 1910 to 1960, included two world wars and their aftermaths. What had been the major scourges of the eighteenth and nineteenth centuries, such as cholera and smallpox, had virtually been eradicated, to be replaced by concern for such infectious diseases as tuberculosis, influenza, diphtheria, whooping cough, measles, rubella, mumps and polio. It was also a period of rapid advances in medical, pharmaceutical and food sciences, with the discovery of vitamins, insulin, penicillin, and so on; with increasing government interventions with the establishment of a Ministry of Health in 1919 and with the National Health Service in 1948; and with a general rise in the standard of living with the growth of the Welfare State.

When it came to advertising ways of promoting health and safety, whether orthodox or quackery, until well into the twentieth century, it was virtually a free-for-all, with only the rare challenge of claims in courts. What government control of such advertising there was, certainly in the early decades, was largely concerned with the placement of advertisements rather than with their contents. It was not until 1917 that the advertising of remedies 'for any condition associated with sexual indulgence' was prohibited; and not until 1939 that a similar ban was introduced for 'so-called' remedies for cancer.

The advertising industry was rather slow to get its act together; it was not until 1920 that it took a more professional turn, when the Advertisers Protection Society, founded in 1900, was replaced

'Hike for Health' Southern Railway poster,
S.P.B. Mais, 1932.

by the Incorporated Society of British Advertisers. It
has largely been a self-regulatory industry from then
on, even when the Advertising Standards Authority
was set up in the 1960s to oversee that claims should
be proven and 'should neither be exaggerated or
misleading'. The Ministry of Health had its first
press officer in 1918, but much government publicity
relating to health, at least up to the establishment
of the Ministry of Information at the start of WWII,
was, as Scott Anthony described it – 'an odd hybrid of
scientific promotion, advertising, political diplomacy,
education and philanthropy'.

In the selection of fifty years of 'health and safety'
advertising all the decades are sampled, but the focus
is largely on the bigger more reputable advertisers
and on government publicity. Such advertisements
and posters may not be open to as much humour
and scoffing as the small press advertisements of the
quacks, but as the book is as much concerned with
the design of advertisements as with their content,
this clearly is better illustrated by organisations with
large budgets.

Nevertheless many of these were tempted, from
time to time, to exaggerate or make unsubstantiated
claims. Giving them the benefit of the doubt, this

'Health and Physical Perfection' booklet produced by Hancock's Chemist, undated.

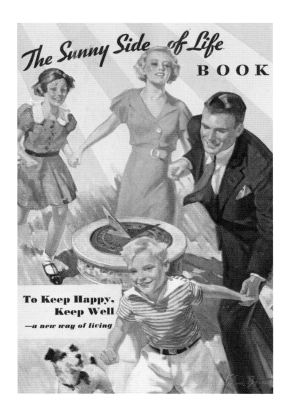

'The Sunny Side of Life' booklet cover, produced by Kellogg's, 1934.

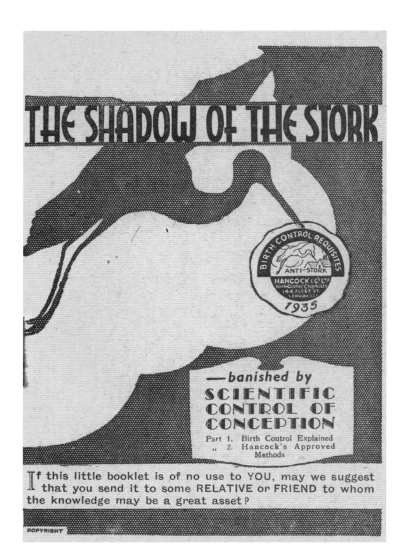

Above: Advert for Allenburys Pastille, Stan Krol, undated. Right: 'The shadow of the stork' booklet, Hancock & Co Ltd chemists, 1935.

could well have related more to the state of scientific knowledge at the time (albeit tinged by a soupçon of optimism) rather than to any conscious attempt to deceive or defraud.

Tobacco advertising is a particularly good example of this as although there had been a tenuous link of smoking to cancer as early as the 1910s, it was not until the 1940s and 50s that the link was firmly established. Yet in the inter-war years not only were some of the best commercial artists employed in advertising tobacco products, but there are examples of claims that smoking was actually beneficial.

The first three sections of this book are largely concerned with examples of government and non-commercial health and safety advertising, the remaining chapters with that of commercial enteprises.

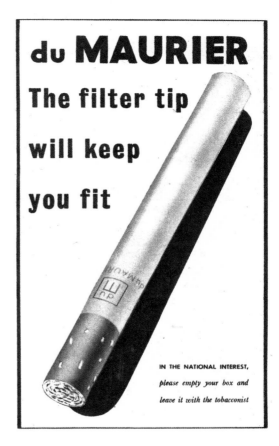

'The filter tip will keep you fit', du Maurier press advertisement, *Picture Post*, February 1941.

GOVERNMENT HEALTH CAMPAIGNS

...we are still losing about 22 million weeks' work each year through common and often preventable illnesses such as colds and influenza, dyspepsia, biliousness, neurasthenia, rheumatism, bois and other septic conditions. This is calculated to be equivalent to the loss of 24,000 tanks, 6,750 bombers, and 6,750,000 rifles a year not to mention the pain and inconvenience we suffer as individuals. We cannot expect, whatever we do, to wipe out this loss completely.

Ministry of Health pamphlet, 1943

It would, in fact, take such events as wars or epidemics, before the British government could conceive of having any responsibility at all for the health of its citizens. Although Sir Thomas More is said to have outlined a plan for a national health service in his *Utopia* of 1524, it was not until the 1830s that the government began to stir itself. Generally people were considered responsible for their own ailments, or, if they were able, they could contribute to a Friendly Society or could seek help from charities or charitable hospitals.

It was in 1837 that it was made mandatory to record, when registering a death, its likely cause, which meant that at least some rudimentary statistics could be built up to guide policy. But it was the crisis arising from the cholera outbreaks in the 1830s that led the government to first appoint Health Boards and medical officers, and, in 1848, a national Board of Health. It was actually a civil servant, Edwin Chadwick, whose report on 'The Sanitary Condition of the Labouring Classes' that triggered the first Public Health Act in 1848, albeit his motives were thought to have been possibly more economic than welfare.

The idea that the government could make public its concerns, could get its messages across by using the know-how of the developing advertising and publicity industries, did not really come into play, to any extent, until just before WWII, albeit there had been a Department/Ministry of Information for a short period at the end of WWI. The exception had been the Post Office publicity, in the hands of the pioneering Stephen Tallents, in the mid-1930s.

The government made a not too successful campaign relating to health in 1937. The British had performed disappointingly at the 1936 Berlin Olympic Games, and the government realized that such movements in Germany as 'Health through joy' were not only intent on building a 'superior' race, but one fit for war. So although the 1937 'Physical Training and Recreation Act' was ostensibly about

'In work or play, fitness wins!' poster campaign, by advertising agents Armstrong-Warden, The National Fitness Council, *c.*1938.

health and fitness, it was very much a catching up exercise. There had, of course, been interest in exercise before this, but this tended to be exercise for character building rather more than for health, as Thomas Arnold's 'muscular Christianity' at Rugby School in the 1850s, Baden Powell's Boy Scouts in 1908, and Kurt Hahn's 'Salem system' at Gordonstoun in the 1930s. Similarly, such movements as the Ramblers' Association, the Youth Hostel Association and the National Playing Fields Association, had concerns other than health, as right of access. Being voluntary bodies they had very limited budgets for advertising, although the National Playing Fields Association, founded by George V in 1925, did commission such luminaries as Austin Cooper and Tom Purvis for a poster campaign in 1927.

The 1937 Act, which set up a National Advisory Council aimed to fund exercise facilities, to encourage local authorities to make provision for physical activities, and generally to raise public awareness of the need 'to be fit'. A massive publicity campaign was launched using not only the press and the hoardings, but radio and film. The Lord Mayor's Show of that year had 'Physical Fitness' as

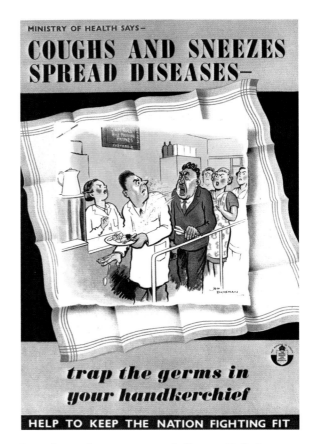

'Coughs and sneezes spread diseases' Ministy of Health poster, Bateman, 1942.

its theme; the British pavilion at the Glasgow Empire Exhibition of 1938 was also themed 'Fitter Britain'. Posters appeared on hoardings with the tag 'Get Fit – Keep Fit'. These were in strip form – the two issued in April and May 1937 were in black and white and featured, respectively, people going around their daily tasks, and men and women playing sport; the third, coming out in June, was in colour, and showed people on holiday. That the government's concern for fitness was fitness to cope with war became evident in its lack of interest in the matter in the immediate post-war years, at least until the 1960 Wolfenden Report on 'Sport and the Community'.

But it was the massive amount of propaganda emerging from Germany in the 1930s that prompted the government to establish its own propaganda machine, which would come to deal with matters of health, along with a whole range of other concerns. Several years in the planning, the Ministry of Information was established on the 4th September 1939 – 'to promote the national case to the public at home and abroad in time of war'.

After a rather sticky start with a number of changes of management, the Ministry settled down to its work under the steadying hand of

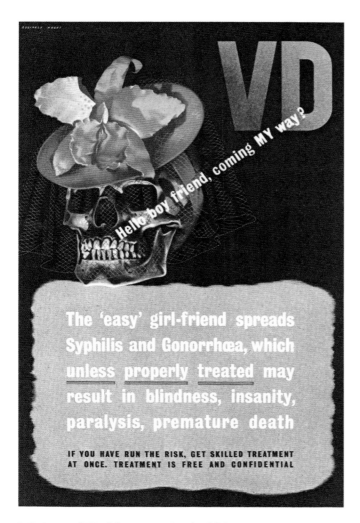

Ministry of Health poster, Reginald Mount, *c.*1943.

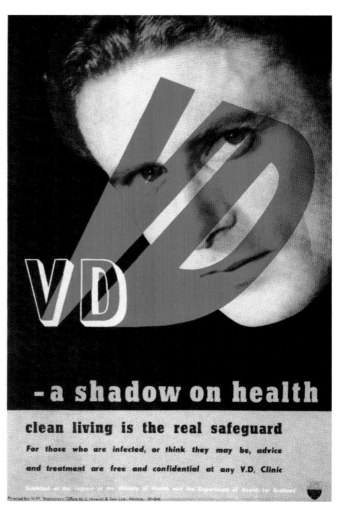

Ministy of Health poster, F.H.K. Henrion, 1943.

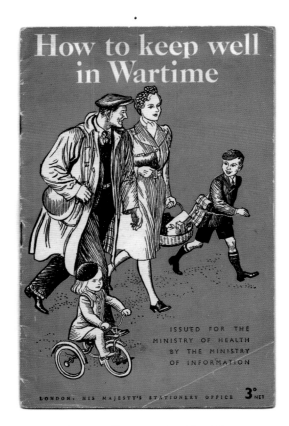

How to keep well
in Wartime

ISSUED FOR THE
MINISTRY OF HEALTH
BY THE MINISTRY
OF INFORMATION

LONDON: HIS MAJESTY'S STATIONERY OFFICE   3º NET

'How to keep well in Wartime' booklet,
issued for the Ministry of Health by the
Ministry of Information, 1943.

Brendon Bracken. The Ministry of Health itself,
or via the Ministry of Information, ran a number
of health campaigns during WWII, on specific
aspects of health, along with general information
on 'keeping well in wartime'. The two health areas
that most concerned the government at this time
were the prevention of venereal disease, and the
encouragement of people to make use of services for
immunization against such diseases as diphtheria.
Other health-related campaigns included appeals
for blood donors, and one for the prevention of
colds and influenza. Particularly worried about
absenteeism and 'helping keeping the nation fighting
fit' the 'Coughs and Sneezes' campaign made much
use of the humour of such artists as Bateman and of
Dorrit Dekk. 'Coughs and sneezes spread diseases'
became common parlance, and was still being used
as late as 1961 when hummed by Tony Hancock in
The Blood Donor.

Although the government was well aware of the
problems of venereal diseases (VD) as early as the
1860s, when a study of its occurrence in troops
led to the police being given the right to imprison
prostitutes who were found to be infected, others
had also interested themselves in the problem.

Christabel Pankhurst who wrote her book 'The Great Scourge and how to end it' in 1913 was particularly evangelical on the subject. Yet it was not until WWI that a Public Health Act was passed, requiring local authorities to set up treatment centres. Other bodies, as the National Council for Controlling Venereal Disease (which became the Social Hygiene Council) and the National Society for the Prevention of Venereal Disease, found difficulty in getting their message across, as the moral stigma was such that much of the press refused to carry VD advertisements.

With WWII came the massive movement of people enlisting in the forces, being evacuated from danger zones, and moving to work in munitions, in pits, and on the land. The possibility of the spread of venereal diseases led pressure to be put on the government to take action, and leaflets, press advertisements, and posters began to appear, breaking through the secrecy that had surrounded the matter. Even so the initial posters tended to be small, containing only official-looking texts, and were placed discreetly in public lavatories. But the campaign of 1942 took a more confident approach, and posters began to appear on railway

Booklet produced by the Ministry of Food, 1943.

stations and in other easily accessible public places. The government set out to treat the problem as a medical rather than a moral one, the church saw it as the latter, and the campaign was, consequently, surrounded with much controversy. Inevitably a moral angle began to creep into the government publicity, which targeted 'loose women' and urged men to protect 'your pure wife and innocent children, the future of the nation'.

The two artists producing some of the most iconic images for these government campaigns were Reginald Mount and F.H.K. Henrion. Mount, who was the senior Ministry of Information artist during WWII, continuing to work for it after the war, produced two particularly threatening anti-VD posters focusing on the 'easy girl friend' and the 'pure bride'. Of the former, an image of a fetching red hat on a skull, Mount wrote – 'I wanted to show that contact with this sort of female could be, quite literally, the kiss of death'. Henrion's also set out to show the menace of the disease, using photomontage, with a dominating 'VD' in red, pressing down on an innocent baby for one, and another with a handsome young man, tagged 'clean living is the real safeguard'. Henrion claimed that

his VD posters were so successful that even young people not suffering from sexually transmitted diseases would turn up at the clinics.

The government's approach to immunisation ran along similarly cautionary lines. It was only with the research of such people as Edward Jenner, Robert Koch and Louis Pasteur that the science of bacteriology developed and the idea that people could be made immune to a number of diseases was eventually accepted.

As early as 1835 a Vaccination Act had been passed making the vaccination of babies up to three months mandatory, extended in 1867 to children up to fourteen. There was continuous opposition to such government interventions, as there still is today, mainly stemming from the fear of the unknown, but also on economic and religious grounds as well. Opposition was so strong by the end of the nineteenth century that a conscientious objection/opt out clause had to be brought in.

By the early years of the twentieth century vaccines had been found for a number of diseases including diphtheria, cholera and polio. Yet by the start of WWII statistics have it that some 50,000 children, mainly under-tens, were still catching

Your Children's FOOD IN WARTIME

You want your children to be healthy and happy, of course; and to grow up strong and sturdy. Do you know that all that depends very largely upon the food you give them now, and the food habits you help them to form? By following the few simple rules given in this leaflet, you can do much to make sure that your children build sound constitutions and healthy, active bodies.

Why is a child's food so vitally important?

1. Because a child develops bones, muscles and teeth entirely from food. Through the mother before birth, and in the diet of early and late childhood.

2. A child's food must also provide for the daily upkeep of the body, for protection against illness and for the supply of energy for almost ceaseless activity.

3. The younger the child, the smaller the quantity of food that can be taken at one meal; therefore each food served must be of good nutritional value.

Foods that build bones, muscle and teeth

1 MILK

A. Take full advantage of the Government's Milk Schemes. See that your child gets all the "priority" milk he or she is entitled to at home, and that school children get milk in school wherever possible.

B. See that each child in the family actually consumes his or her full allowance of milk, and that it is not given to any grown-up.

C. Use the National Household Skimmed Milk as an extra when it is obtainable.

D. Use milk in vegetable soups and stews, as well as in puddings, sauces and drinks.

WAR COOKERY LEAFLET 10

MINISTRY OF FOOD

Ministry of Food leaflet, No. 10, undated.

SUGGESTIONS for BREAKFAST

A GOOD BREAKFAST EVERY DAY IS THE FIRST RULE IN THE BOOK OF HEALTH

Get up early enough to enjoy breakfast without hurry. A cup of tea and a morsel of toast gulped down with one eye on the clock is no use to anyone. Breakfast is an important meal for all of us, but especially important for growing school children and young factory workers.

MINISTRY OF FOOD
LEAFLET
No. 33

Ministry of Food leaflet, No. 33, 1939.

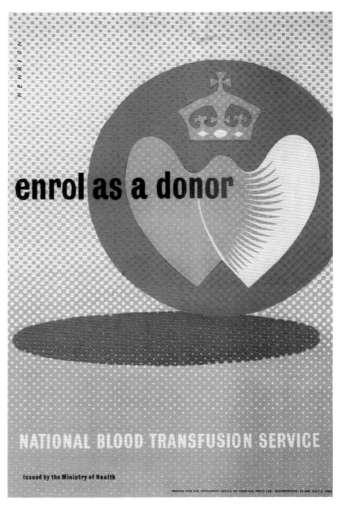

Ministry of Health advertisement, *Housewife*, 1944.

Ministy of Health poster, F.H.K. Henrion, 1947.

diphtheria annually, resulting in some 2–3,000 deaths.

It was just prior to the start of WWII that the Ministry of Health brought in its mass immunisation scheme for diphtheria, and, between 1942 and 1944 launched a major propaganda campaign stressing the fatal consequences of parents choosing not to immunise their children. The threat of likely death from such neglect was repeatedly employed, with slogans as 'Diphtheria is Deadly' and 'Diphtheria costs Lives'. With the publicity there was added reassuring notes that the procedure was entirely safe, simple, and quick (only 2 or 3 jabs), and free. Occasionally the Ministry resorted to using heavy weights of 'medical science' to support their cause, as in an advertisement in *Housewife* in 1944 – 'The Children's Doctor at Guy's Hospital says…'. As immunization for further diseases was added to the Ministry's concern, advertisements became more general just headed 'Protect your Child' but listing polio, tetanus and smallpox along with diphtheria as targets.

SAFETY

Health & Safety has, perhaps, become something of a butt for jibes these days, with local as well as national interventions in people's lives in this respect considered overprotective. But this is after a long history of very necessary government interventions eventually being made to combat the worst effects of the industrial revolution. From the 1802 Act for the Preservation of the Health and Morals of Apprentices and the appointment of factory inspectors in the 1830s, to a further series of Factory Acts throughout the rest of the nineteenth century and well into the twentieth, the government widened its safety and health concerns to other work places, as mines, railways, shipping and agriculture; both work accidents and the prevention of industrial diseases were addressed.

And the government became increasingly concerned about safety elsewhere, particularly on the roads. There had been a Highway Act as early as 1835 relating to carts and carriages, but it was with the arrival of the motorcar, towards the end of the century, that the government became really active in relation to road safety; the first Motor Car Act was passed in 1896. By 1919 there was a Ministry of Transport in place, and there followed, intermittently, throughout the twentieth century, further legislation affecting speed of transport, licences to drive, and so on.

From time to time the government launched campaigns to encourage certain behaviours and to prevent others, and these would be accompanied by press advertisements, posters, leaflets and exhibitions. An example is Hans Schleger's designs

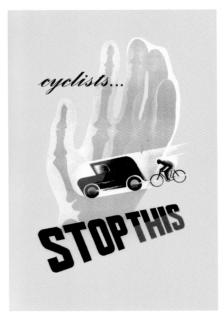

and iconic poster for the Ministry's 'Highway Code' exhibition at Charing Cross Underground Station in 1937. WWII brought with it the additional road hazards, when street lighting was restricted, of moving around in the blackout. The Ministry, sometimes in cooperation with the Royal Society for the Prevention of Accidents (RoSPA), produced a plethora of relevant posters warning pedestrians to ensure that they were clearly seen by drivers by wearing or carrying something white. A particularly lurid series, in blue and pink, carrying such a message, designed by Tom Gentleman, was issued by London Transport.

Safety posters and advertisements, whether related to preventing accidents in the home, at work, or on the road, were not only put out by government departments, RoSPA, and London Transport, but by other employers as the railway companies, and by commercial enterprises, as ICI. The Post Office, which had carved out such a distinguished position when it came to commissioning good art for publicity purposes when Stephen Tallents had been its first

Publicity Manager in the 1930s, employed a number of well-known artists and designers for its own inhouse safety posters, as Stan Krol, Hans Unger, Paxton Chadwick and David Langdon.

But the organisation most energetic in working to protect people from what it considered avoidable accidents and illnesses was RoSPA. The British Industrial 'Safety First' Association came into being at the end of WWI, dropping the word 'British' from its title in 1923, and eventually settling for RoSPA in 1941. Although much of its early work related to road accidents, with a particular focus on educating children to good kerb drill, it was very soon running campaigns, holding competitions, issuing booklets and posters on all aspects of safety, supported in its evangelism by its considerable research on actual accident statistics. From its start RoSPA worked closely with the government, having government representatives on its board, and cooperating on campaigns with both the Ministry of Transport and the Ministry of Labour.

Of all the 'For your health' initiatives, whether selling patent medicines, or disinfectants or cereals, whether by government, local government, voluntary organisations or commercial firms,

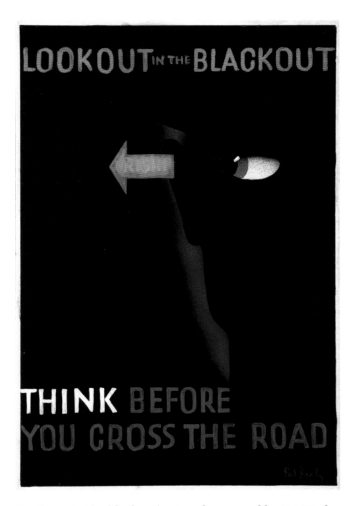

'Look out in the blackout', artwork proposal by Pat Keely for a poster for RoSPA, *c.*1940.

DON'T
walk near
edge of platform
SAFETY FIRST

LNER poster, Arthur Watts, 1924.

mind
that
door

opening carriage doors before the train stops
CAUSES ACCIDENTS

please stand away from platform edge

BRITISH RAILWAYS

British Railways poster, Tom Eckersley, 1961.

RoSPA, in its zeal, probably commissioned some of the best artists and produced some of the most outstanding publicity.

Some of its posters actually found their way to the New York Museum of Modern Art, well before the sniffy British galleries and museums would touch anything quite so vulgar. During the years covered by this book, RoSPA used dozens of artists, including Abram Games, Manfred Reiss, Hans Schleger and H.A. Rothholz. The most frequently commissioned were Leonard Cusden, Pat Keely, and, perhaps more than any other, Tom Eckersley. Eckersley was to produce some twenty two posters for RoSPA during WWII alone, whilst working in the RAF, his contribution being recognised by his being awarded the OBE. His posters sent their message forcibly by their simplicity, using less than half a dozen words and a stark image along the lines – 'Replace covers, Prevent falls'.

Pat Keely designed safety posters for both the Post Office and for RoSPA. His work had a similar simplicity to that of Eckersley – 'Stack tidily and safely', 'Gear Wheels catch clothes', 'Don't set traps', and so on. Keely, a sadly neglected artist of considerable merit, did a number of safety posters

'How to be Safe' booklet, issued by RoSPA, Emil Weiss, 1948.

DON'T LISTEN TO THE TRAFFIC JIMP

"Why go round?" says the Traffic Jimp. "You can cross here, can't you?"

Perhaps you can. But each scurry across is a risk you needn't take.

On a pedestrian crossing, drivers are *expecting* you. Here, they're not. So it's more difficult for them, more dangerous for you. Jay-walking is one of the reasons why 2,380 pedestrians were killed last year. 52,850 were injured.

The Traffic Jimp tempts you to try and save time. Don't listen. Using the crossings may *save your life*.

Issued by the Ministry of Transport

Above: Press advertisement, Ministry of Transport, *Lilliput*, 1949. **Right:** Ministry of Transport advert, *Boys Own Paper*, June 1950.

Brilliant England centre-forward, the 'wisest head in Soccer' . . .

Tommy Lawton SAYS

"Here's how I cross roads . ."

" Fancy foot-work scores on the football-field, where you want to confuse the other side's halves and backs. But on the road, confusion is the last thing you want. *Head*-work is the thing, when you're crossing a street. Here's how *I* do it :

1 At the kerb—HALT.
2 Eyes—RIGHT.
3 Eyes—LEFT.
4 Glance again—RIGHT.
5 If all clear—QUICK MARCH.
   Quite calm, no running and dodging, because I wait for a proper gap in the traffic first.

" If you misjudge things in Soccer — well, you're very seldom hurt, anyway. But if you take chances in *traffic*, you may be *killed*. And the same accident may kill others. So watch your step, be a good Road Navigator and cross all streets the Kerb Drill way."

T. Lawton

Issued by the Ministry of Transport

for the Post Office, particularly relating to coping with wartime blackout. Leonard Cusden, yet another now largely forgotten artist, who had produced posters for the railways in the 1930s, produced some of RoSPA's most iconic images as 'Beware the Swarf' and 'Let's Have a Safety Record to Shout About'. A variation of the message RoSPA was trying to put across, was the strip cartoon misadventures of Percy Vere, devised by Philip Mendoza. A curiosity worth mentioning, as being a rarity, one by a woman, was Grace Golden's WWII 'Keep your Mind on your Job and save your Knuckles'. In all, the RoSPA archives hold well over seven hundred safety posters, as Dr. Paul Rennie had declared – 'a testimony to a long and continuous effort to improve the quality of working and everyday life for ordinary people'.

Keep You
HEALTHY
HAPPY
and
SLIM

Obtainable Everywhere
in PENNY TWISTS & 6ᴰ
1/3 and 3/- Packs

PATENT MEDICINES

How often do we come across young ladies who lead indolent lives, and who, for lack of some healthy physical and mental employment, occupy their time in thinking of themselves and nursing any little bodily or nervous weakness that may ail them till their attention becomes so absorbed with their self and their trivial complaints that these become magnified in their eye to such a degree that they are actually led to believe they are really victims of disease and are surrounded by unsympathetic friends.

Robert Bell, M.D., 1903

The patient responds to the suggestion made by the advertiser or prescriber and gets better because he believes in the potential efficiency of the product he's taking rather than because of any inherent qualities of the drug ... It is a sad but true fact that if you fill a bottle with coloured water and call it the Elixir of Life people will buy it by the gallon.
Dr. Vernon Coleman, 1980

In his book *The Home Pharmacy*, published some thirty years ago, Dr. Coleman complained of the difficulty of even listing the myriad of home remedies, let alone of trying to differentiate between seemingly competing brands. He had found some 150 claimed remedies for colds alone, caustically commenting 'I doubt if the disappearance of all of them would have had any effect on the health of

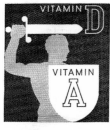

ARM YOURSELF–
GUARD YOURSELF!

Make <u>sure</u> of your daily vitamins

You must have them. You must have them *regularly*. And you must have a *sufficiency* of them. Otherwise you cannot get and keep that abundant good health you ought to be enjoying.

You need Vitamin A to help protect your body against infection. You need Vitamin D to strengthen your body's framework and build healthy teeth. But where can you be *certain* of finding them?

Three years ago a wonderful discovery, brought to perfection at the famous Crookes Laboratories, established Halibut Liver Oil as the richest known natural source of these two vitamins. Immediately the whole medical profession accepted Crookes' Halibut Liver Oil as a sovereign preparation for building up both adults and children after illness, correcting many of their weaknesses, and warding off chills and other ailments. When it is remembered that the chief virtue of cod liver oil lies in its Vitamin A and D content, the significance of the following fact becomes apparent :—

There is 80 times more Vitamin A in Crookes' Halibut Liver Oil than in the finest ★ cod liver oil, and 30-40 times more Vitamin D

★ *This means over 300 times more Vitamin A than in average cod liver oil.*

You can take this oil either in liquid form or in capsu'es. Either way you are certain of getting the same high and *standardised* vitamin content ; the green label the carton is your guarantee of this. Take Crookes' regularly this winter, and give it to your children. It strengthens and protects without fattening, and even the most squeamish can assimilate it with ease.

A single drop of Crookes' Halibut Liver Oil is equal to a teaspoonful of finest cod liver oil.

CROOKES'
PURE HALIBUT LIVER
OIL
'COLLOSOL' BRAND (Regd.)

In liquid form, with dropper, per phial containing sixteen days' full adult dosage 2/-. In capsule form, per bottle of 25 capsules, each containing a full dose 2/6. Of all chemists.

There are three other preparations of Crookes' Halibut Liver Oil : HALIMALT, HALYCITROL and HALYCALCYNE. *The Crookes Laboratories, Park Royal, London, N.W.10*

FROM THESE DEEP WATERS
COMES A WEAPON TO FIGHT DISEASE

In the deep-water seas of Greenland, Iceland and the North Pacific the halibut swims along the ocean bed. And scientists discovered that within the halibut are stored two vitamins which together form one of the most potent aids to health known to man. For halibut oil is a richly concentrated source of vitamins A and D, without which it is impossible for adults to maintain health or children to grow up with straight bones and strong teeth.

The Crookes Laboratories are proud to be associated with the work of these doctors and scientists — proud to supply them with the means to fight disease and to bring health and happiness into the lives of ordinary people.

CROOKES MAKERS OF VITAMIN PRODUCTS

THE CROOKES LABORATORIES LIMITED · PARK ROYAL · LONDON · NW10

the nation.' In taking a stab at the number of home remedies then on the market he hazarded 24,000, and wrote enviously of the Egyptians who had confidently noted only 975. He warned his readers that home medicines were big business and urged a healthy skepticism when they were considering advertising claims.

A satisfactory account of the history of patent medicines and their claims would require a volume or more, and here is a quite arbitrary selected handful, with interesting images or copy, or both, when the majority of patent medicine advertisements for the period covered by this book tended to be a few lines, crammed into a single column of a newspaper or magazine, in small type and very rarely illustrated except by the odd 'fakir', or the like.

One group of illustrated patent medicines that were advertised frequently, some still major players today, were the 'liver oils', said to be useful in 'detoxifying the blood', and later, sometimes adding, 'building strong bones and teeth in the young'. Fish oil was a traditional remedy around the coasts of Scandinavia and Newfoundland, where, according to folk custom, fish liver, dowsed in sea water, would be

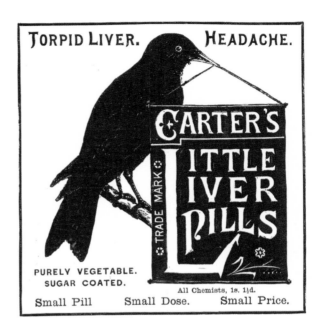

Carter's Little Liver Pills advert, undated.

allowed to ferment for long periods before the oil was drawn off; that in Newfoundland this same oil was also used as a paint ingredient, could not have been entirely reassuring.

It was not until the 1920s, with the progress in vitamin research, that high profiling of the product began in earnest, the major competitors being Crookes' Halibut Oil (produced in Hull), and Seven

Tom Eckersley poster for Seven Seas, 1947.

'Your birthright is health' Eno's advert, undated.

Seas Cod Liver Oil (based in Park Royal, London), both claiming the remedial effects of vitamins A and D in their products. Whether the two fish sources had similar effects was not spelt out, although one Crookes' advertisement, in 1935, claimed that its product had 80 times more vitamin A than the finest cod's liver; only later it was found that an excess of this vitamin could in fact be harmful.

Crookes' advertisements tended to run along fairly traditional lines, oftimes resorting to the typical military language that so many remedies had adopted, as 'arm yourself – guard yourself'. By the 1940s and '50s merely a hand holding a tiny pill

was considered sufficient to show off the product, perhaps to reassure purchasers of the ease of ingesting it.

Seven Seas had started out as the British Cod Liver Oil producers, a cooperative venture of Hull Trawler owners, seeking to make optimum use of their catch. It was Kenneth MacLenman, an ex-Lever Bros. man, appointed as manager in 1936, who coined the brand name Seven Seas. Again, its advertising was fairly common stuff until, in the 1940s and '50s it commissioned Tom Eckersley. Eckersley broke ground, using bold colours, and replacing smiling adults and children with few allusions to the sea, by humorous images of stylized

Neptunes and muscle bulging sailors, with the tag 'the sea-fresh vitamin food'.

Probably the most consistently good advertising design for liver ailments during the first half of the twentieth century, was that for Eno's Fruit Salts. James Crossley Eno, a Newcastle chemist, set up his 'Fruit Salt Works' in south east London in the 1850s. From the start he marketed his product for –

any constitutional weakness of the liver, for it possesses the power of regeneration when digestion has been disturbed or lost and places the invalid on the right track to health.

and further –

Eno's 'Fruit Salt' encourages the system to debarrass itself of the waste which will otherwise accumulate and spoil temper, health, breath, skin – everything.

Initially Eno's advertising was similar to other peddlers of such wares – crowded with words of advice, moral as well as medical, occasionally accompanied by an image of a fair maiden clearly benefiting from the product. A sea change occurred when Crawford's advertising agency was retained when the company felt a need for a fresh start after WWI, the field left clear by the death of Eno in 1915. Crawford's brought modernism into advertising

Advertisement for Eno's Fruit Salt, Edward McKnight Kauffer, 1924.

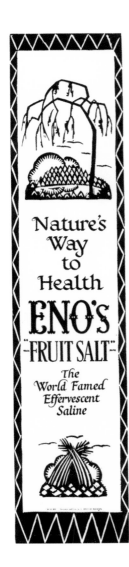

Nature's
Way
to
Health

ENO'S
"FRUIT SALT"

The
World Famed
Effervescent
Saline

Keep fit
in
Winter

drink

ENO'S
"FRUIT SALT"

The
World Famed
Effervescent
Saline

'MORNING BOB!'

Come on Slow-coach
Show a leg
Can't you smell the
Ham and egg?
Breakfast's ready, Bob!
What—you'll sleep.
A long while yet?
Nonsense, man!
Rouse up and get
Eno on the job!

Find your Eno
Sleepy head:
Eno gets you
Out of bed
Fit for work or play.
Sparkling Eno
When you rise,
Cleans your blood,
Clears your eyes,
Ready for the day.

ENO FOR HEALTH AND HAPPINESS
ENO FIRST THING EVERY MORNING

Eno's Fruit Salt is sold all over the world.

Left: Two from a series of woodcut press advertisements for Eno's, Dillon McGurk, 1925. **Above:** Press advert for Eno's, Ashley Havinden, *Punch*, June 1927. **Right:** Advert for Eno's, George Whitelaw, 1932.

for patent medicines with the employment of such greats as McKnight Kauffer and Ashley Havinden, neither of them much shakes when it came to actual drawing, but both outstanding designers with colour, typography and layout. Kauffer's cockerel crowing in the morning for Eno's, came to be seen everywhere, on posters, in press advertisements and in shop displays. Sir Lawrence Weaver, the distinguished sponsor and critic of design in the 1920s wrote of it –

Mr. Snooks (Everyman) may be puzzled rather than pleased by Mr. Kauffer's suggestion of how a rooster shall present its tail feathers to the public eye, but he may yet remember what it means in relation to the first thing in the morning and to the duty of which Sir William Crawford's young men write with so much delicacy and persuasion.

Ashley's three horsemen, riding into battle, came to be just as frequently seen as Kauffer's rooster; but he also went on to create many other advertisements for Eno's in the inter-war years, particularly striking being his full-page ones appearing weekly in Punch, characterized as they were by much use of white space and originality of typography and layout. *Commercial Art*, in 1928 wrote of Ashley's work for Eno's –

In many quarters in England it is held that modernity in art is either wicked or weak-minded, and is in any case a ruinous attribute. At least one is often told this though I have never personally witnessed a popular outburst of indignation in front of Mr. Ashley Havinden's Eno's Fruit Salt poster.

Crawford's was to continue as Eno's agent through to the 1960s, with later noteworthy campaigns, such as George Whitelaw's 'The Can and Can't family', and the Bert Thomas's 'Whose been at my Eno's?' series of twelve posters in 1938 of which he wrote –

First you laugh at one; then you saw another one and laughed about what was really the same joke

Who's been at my
ENO'S
?

ENO'S 'FRUIT SALT,' famous during 5 reigns

the words 'Eno' and 'Fruit Salt' are registered trade-marks

Left: Press advertisement for Eno's, Bert Thomas, *Punch*, March 1937. **Above:** 'Every morning take Eno's fruit salt' advert, *c*.1945.

dressed up in a different way.

   Another genre of patent medicines that were widely advertised but with nowhere near the panache of Eno's, was that group claiming to have laxative effects, the two most high-profile being Beecham's Pills and Bile Beans. Beecham's Pills, 'working quietly and gently overnight', were developed by Thomas Beecham, a young market trader in his twenties, describing himself as 'Chemist, Druggist and Tea Dealer'. By 1847 he was licensed to sell medicines and was developing a range of his own, including his pills. These he manufactured and sold direct, as well as by mail order, from his factory in St. Helens. He pushed his pills as 'cure-alls', said to tackle, amongst other ailments, fullness and swelling after meals, shortness of breath, cold chills and giddiness.

   By 1895 Thomas had retired and his son James, an enthusiastic marketer, took over. James, who appears to have been something of a heavyweight (Mayor of St. Helens and knighted), particularly developed the advertising side of the business, to the extent that Beecham's Pills became one of the largest advertisers in the inter-war years. The name for the product was, even when it was no longer a family

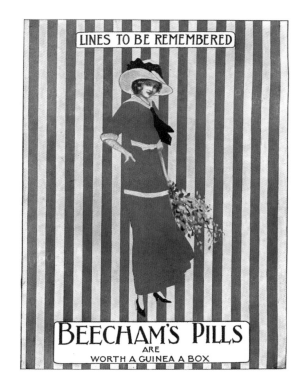

'Lines to be remembered – Beecham's Pills are worth a guinea a box' press advertisement for Beecham's, undated.

All Sorts & Conditions.
of People in every "walk" of Life
appreciate the Wonderful Powers of –
BEECHAMS PILLS.
WORTH A GUINEA A BOX

Left: Press advert for Beecham's Pills, undated. **Opposite left:** Beecham's first poster for the hoardings, 1938. **Opposite centre:** Beecham's advert, undated. **Opposite right:** Beecham's advert, *Picture Post*, April 1953.

firm, but became Beecham's Pharmaceuticals, giving it a shade more prestige.

During WWI Beecham's, in its advertising, went all out to associate itself with wartime patriotism devising a series of semi-humorous advertisements, some by the popular artist Bruce Bairnsfather, provided when he was actually at the front, and later when he was invalided out. He recorded sketching 'in six inches of mud and water at the bottom of my dug-out'.

A typical Bairnsfather WWI advertisement for Beecham's shows a soldier firing a machine gun with the caption 'Maxim to Remember. Beecham's Pills will keep you up to the mark.' Bairnsfather actually initialled his work, but generally artists producing advertisements for Beecham's, as in so much commercial art, went unacknowledged.

James Beecham concentrated on using the press and was strongly against hoardings, and it was not until 1938 that the tradition was broken. Its first hoarding poster, devised by the agency Sir John Couston & Sons Ltd., was of the simplest – a rosy cheeked smiling girl's head with 'Health, Energy and Happiness' blaring out above what had become

the company's usual tag for its pills – 'worth a guinea a box'.

Bile Beans boasted an even greater spread when it came to the ailments it could remedy –

...headaches, influenza, scrofula, piles, liver trouble, bad breath, fullness after eating, constipation, lack of ambition, flatulence, debility, female ailments, pimples, rheumatism, indigestion, dizziness, anaemia, ulcers and buzzing in the head.

Bile Beans was originally marketed as 'Gould's Tiny Tonic Pills', and then 'Charlie Forde's Bile Beans'. Charles Fulford, a Canadian, who had worked for a time in a chemist's shop and was interested in vegetable remedies, in 1896 met up with an Englishman, Ernest Gilbert, who was running a stationery shop in New South Wales, Australia. The two thought up the concoction, which they advertised as 'Bile Beans for Biliousness'.

With Bile Beans as the brand name the business flourished and soon there were factories in the United States and in Leeds. Although Fulford had been challenged as to whether there actually was anyone called Charlie Forde, and as to whether Fulford was the distinguished scientist he claimed to

'For 1940 – be fit & slim by taking Bile Beans' advert, *Picture Post*, December 1939.

'Bile Beans keep you healthy, happy and slim', paper bag, undated.

be, and as to whether the product was vegetable or, indeed, had any healing qualities at all, by 1905 it was selling throughout the world. Bile Beans was eventually found to be truly a laxative, and continued to be produced as such in Leeds, through to the 1960s, when the company was acquired by Fisons.

Advertising claims seem to have become increasingly vague as the years went on, and, by the late 1930s 'slimness' had been added to 'fitness' – an attractive cosmetic effect added to the otherwise more earthy laxative attribute – 'Bile Beans for Radiant Health and a Lovely Figure'.

'Why is it healthier to be slim' press advert, *Picture Post*, February 1941.

CEREALS
Breakfast foods and bread

It has been claimed that learning to grow cereals triggered hunter-gatherers to become cultivators, which, in turn, was to lead to the urbanization of civilisations. A rather more modest claim has been that the consumption of cereals is essential for good health, whether 'puffed, flaked, flavoured, shaped, sugared, salted or extruded'.

That cereals have become a common breakfast food for the British is almost entirely due to American evangelism, both for our morals and for our health. As early as the 1830s, the Reverend Sylvester Graham declared that the consumption of meat raised undesirable carnal appetites, whereas whole wheat flour had an altogether more calming quality. By the 1860s James Caleb Jackson had developed a wheat based breakfast cereal, Granula, which was served at his health spa in Battle Creek, Michigan.

But it was the brothers Kellogg – Dr. John Harvey and Will Keith – in their own Battle Creek Sanatorium, working on the hypothesis that constipation was related to lack of fibre, who developed a range of grain based cereals that were not only marketed as good for one's health, but unlike Jackson's bran, actually tasted good. By the turn of the century Battle Creek has been described as a cereal Klondike with over one hundred cereal factories! Kellogg's Corn Flakes were launched in 1898 and Kellogg's All Bran in 1916. A London office was set up in 1924, and, in 1928, Kellogg's had its own manufacturing plant in Trafford Park, Manchester.

Of course there were many other cereal manufacturers who also found Britain a ready market – Henry Perky of Colorado, invented a

THE ROAD TO REGULARITY

Above: Booklet, issued by the Kellogg Company, 1934. **Right:** Kellogg's press advertisement, 1929. **Far right:** Kellogg's press advertisement, *Housewife*, June 1944.

machine that would convert wheat into a cushioned biscuit and was marketing the resultant product as Shredded Wheat in 1895. By 1926 the company had established a factory in Welwyn Garden City and the product became Welgar Shredded Wheat. The Quaker Oats Company, which, among other products manufactured Porridge Oats, was yet again American, starting up in Ohio; and even the Australians were in on the act, when Bennison Osborne's Weet-bix came onto the market in the mid-1920s. Its brand name became Weetabix, and it was manufactured in a plant in Burton Latimer, Northamptonshire, opening in 1932.

The advertising of cereals as 'healthy' breakfast foods, at least those using wheat, focused on the fact that the whole grain, the germ and the outer coat, were being used, providing roughage and nutriments. Weetabix, for example, declared it was 'the whole grain, malted, salted and roasted'. The main health advantage of eating cereals was generally given as preventing constipation, most advertisements including the word, but few going into any detail of how this actually was achieved. One rare Kellogg All-Bran wartime advertisement, however, did offer a coy sort of explanation –

399

What shall I give him that's sure to please?

Golden Corn Flakes and sliced bananas

Going out?...no time to cook?... yet he must find a good meal when he comes home.....

Just shake out a bowlful of crisp, tempting golden flakes—slice in a ripe banana—add cold milk or cream and you have a delicious meal prepared in a few seconds. No cooking required. Sold by all grocers in the Red and Green packet.

Kellogg's CORN FLAKES

Made by
KELLOGG *in* LONDON, CANADA
KELLOGG COMPANY of
GREAT BRITAIN, Ltd.
329, High Holborn,
London, W. C. 1.

Also makers of Kellogg's ALL-BRAN   940

SUCCESS STORY

SORRY, BETTY, I'M TOO FAGGED OUT TO GO DANCING. I'VE TRIED DOZENS OF REMEDIES. NOTHING HELPS MY CONSTIPATION

BUT SUE, DARLING, THIS IS DIFFERENT. IT'S A FOOD— NOT A MEDICINE

BETTY SAYS THIS ALL-BRAN WILL HELP MY TROUBLE. IT'S REALLY TASTY. I CAN'T THINK OF A BETTER BREAKFAST

── THREE WEEKS LATER ──

WHY, SUE, YOU LOOK POSITIVELY RADIANT!

THANKS TO YOU AND ALL-BRAN, I FEEL WONDERFUL. NOT A TRACE OF MY OLD TROUBLE LEFT

IF you're constipated, it's probably due to lack of bulk in your diet.

Your food gets almost completely absorbed into the system and the waste matter left behind in the intestines is not bulky enough for the muscles to " take hold of." They cease to work, you get constipated.

Doctors recommend All-Bran, *a natural bulk food.* By supplying the bulk that muscles need to take hold of, All-Bran brings about a thorough and natural movement. Eat All-Bran for breakfast, drink plenty of fluids and say good-bye to constipation. Grocers all over the country have Kellogg's All-Bran. 7½d. a packet, 3 points.

Kellogg's ALL-BRAN

7

First
FOR HEALTH AND VITALITY!

WELGAR SHREDDED WHEAT

(REGISTERED TRADE MARK)

● Health and vitality are chiefly maintained by the food we eat. Welgar Shredded Wheat is the whole wheat and is therefore rich in those food elements that build up sturdy bodies and create the energy necessary for arduous work. It needs no cooking, so is invaluable to those who need a nourishing breakfast quickly.

● *Welgar Shredded Wheat is now zoned in order to save transport. Consequently in some districts it will be unobtainable until normal distribution can be resumed.*

Food for General Fitness

Made by THE SHREDDED WHEAT CO. LIMITED
WELwyn GARden City, Hertfordshire

Your food gets almost completely absorbed into the system and the waste matter left behind in the intestines is not bulky enough 'to take hold of'… All-Bran is the natural bulk food…

As has been mentioned, there were religious origins to some of the breakfast cereals. That Quaker Oats, from its start up in 1877, used the image of a Quaker, thought to be that of William Penn, and described by the company as 'the standard bearer of the Quakers and of Quaker Oats', was rather a matter of association with no direct link between the product and the man, his likeness having been chosen as it represented purity, honesty, strength and other similarly desirable qualities. The association with 'Purity' was also used by other cereal advertisers, as when Weetabix ran a series, using the ditty 'Monday's Child', featuring fresh-faced innocent young girls.

'Purity', usually symbolised by the colour white, was just the reverse when it came to bread, bread advertisements extolling as they did the pure health giving qualities of brown bread. One, Dr. Aslett Baldwin, in an address to the Royal Society of Medicine (undated) declared –

The use of fine white bread and flour is one of the

The Seven Ages of Man

all demand constant nourishment. The better you nourish yourself the longer will you put off old age.

Consider your food and be wise. The more carefully you consider it the more Quaker Oats you will eat, because

Quaker Oats

is the most delicate, most digestible, most up-building, most up-holding, and most economical food in the world. Science and experience prove it to be so.

IT MAKES MOST PORRIDGE. IT MAKES BEST PORRIDGE.

At all Grocers'. In 1 lb. and 2 lb. packets only.

Picture Post, February 18, 1939

Five Smart Girls

– see how the Quins have grown on QUAKER

FIVE merry little Dionnes; healthy, happy and *sturdy* because they've been brought up on Quaker. Their own doctor, who knows the whys and wherefores of the goodness in Quaker, has made the same choice as millions of mothers who know that Quaker is *good* for the kiddies. The Quins get delicious creamy Quaker *every day* without fail. And look what it's done for them!

QUAKER'S TONIC VITAMIN B

Vitamin B is absolutely essential to young and old. Your own doctor will tell you that you must have your Vitamin B *regularly*, for the body can't store it. And what's the most delicious way to get it? *Quaker Oats!*

Quaker is a rich, economical source of Vitamin B, as well as muscle-building

protein, phosphorus and iron. No wonder countless wise mothers are building up sound, sturdy constitutions for their young ones on Quaker every morning.

QUICK QUAKER BREAKFAST

Quick Quaker's the quickest hot breakfast —takes only 4 minutes to prepare. And it's a *real* breakfast—not just cold cereal warmed up with hot milk. Quaker is delicious, creamy, and sustaining. Set yourself up for the day with Quaker; build up the kiddies' constitutions; give the whole family a wholesome delicious Vitamin B *breakfast every day*. And start tomorrow! Get a packet from your grocer!

Join the QUAKER health parade!

40 VITALISING BREAKFASTS FOR 8½d

Future Captain of England at breakfast

He <u>could</u> be your own son

Every successful man owes a lot to his upbringing and a very great many have been brought up on hot nourishing Quaker Oats. Porridge means so much because it gives so much—good wholesome protein to build you up, AND energy and warmth to help you through the cold grey days of winter, AND Vitamin B! (important for digestion and nerves) . . . yes, *everything* in Quaker Oats does you good.

Help your husband, too, with nourishing Quaker Oats . . . to do his job better by seeing he is properly cared for, well-nourished, warm and happy. **1/9½ & 1/0½**

WHATEVER YOU WANT THEM ALL TO BE
They'll do much better on QUAKER

Nurse Busy-bonnet (*such a healthy, jolly young nurse*) always has Weetabix (*and she insists on it for her patients !*)

Mothers too, find that this delicious whole-wheat breakfast cereal gives them — and all the family — that vital morning " staying power." It is, besides, the most economical of all breakfast foods.

Weetabix

A change for breakfast... for snacks, too.

Far left: Quaker Oats press advertisement, undated. **Left:** Weetabix advertisement, *c.*1950s. **Below:** A pair of press adverts for Weetabix, undated.

'Tuesday's child is full of grace'

Monday's child is fair of face
Tuesday's child is full of grace
Wednesday's child is full of woe
Thursday's child has far to go
Friday's child is loving and giving
Saturday's child works hard for his living
But the child that is born on the Sabbath day
Is bonny and blithe and good and gay.

Every line of her lissome and lovely figure is vibrant with the sheer joy of living! Such energy and happiness—the birthright of *all* children—emerge naturally from normal good health. How can this priceless boon be assured—and how safeguarded throughout the trying months of winter? No deep, impenetrable mystery here! The answer is simply . . . *good nutrition.* Encourage children to eat plenty of what they most enjoy . . . plenty of nourishing food . . . as much Weetabix as you can get and give them! Children not only relish the crunchy, nutty flavour of Weetabix, but gain from its whole-wheat goodness the sparkling eyes and animation of healthy and happy childhood.

Weetabix
MORE *than a Breakfast Food*

SMALL SIZE
2 POINTS 7½ᴰ

LARGE SIZE
4 POINTS 1/1ᴰ

Zoned, like all cereals, but perhaps YOU live in a Weetabix area
WX51   WEETABIX LTD., BURTON LATIMER, NORTHANTS

'Monday's Child is Fair of Face'

Monday's child is fair of face
Tuesday's child is full of grace
Wednesday's child is full of woe
Thursday's child has far to go
Friday's child is loving and giving
Saturday's child works hard for his 'living
But the child that is born on the Sabbath day
Is bonny and blithe and good and gay.

Such radiant beauty, the birthright of *every* child, is the outward reflection of perfect health. Weetabix, the delicious whole wheat cereal food, not only builds the foundation of health and energy but helps to keep at bay the ills of winter-time.

Weetabix
MORE *than a Breakfast Food*

SMALL SIZE
2 POINTS 7½ᴰ

LARGE SIZE
4 POINTS 1/1ᴰ

Zoned, like all cereals, but perhaps YOU live in a Weetabix area
WX50   WEETABIX LTD., BURTON LATIMER, NORTHANTS

Above: Advertisement for Hovis Bread, early twentieth century. **Right:** Advertisement for Hovis from *Punch*, April 1938. **Far right:** 'Eat more bread' press advert, 1930.

chief causes of degeneration of the physique and health of civilised communities.

Bread, which has been the staple diet for much of mankind for thousands of years, became, in modern times, the subject of a marketing battle between 'white' and 'brown'. Paradoxically, by the late Middle Ages 'white' was considered the superior, not for its health-giving qualities, for these were unknown at the time, but because it was eaten by the nobility as 'refined'; whilst the poor were only able to afford brown or bran loaves. In this respect the poor were in fact better fed.

Although when one thinks 'brown' one immediately thinks Hovis, it was Allinson's bread, made from Allinson's flour that was one of the first to be stridently sold as essential for healthy eating. In 1899, Thomas Allinson, a London naturopath, a vegetarian and non-smoker, wrote what is probably the first book on the subject entitled 'The Advantages of Whole Wheat Bread', and was actually struck off the list by the Royal College of Physicians for his eccentric notions, which he had written about in 1885 in his book 'A System of Hygenic Medicine'. Being unaccepted by the orthodox in no way curbed his enthusiasm. He had previously bought a stone grinding mill in Bethnal Green, run by his Natural Food Company, and having, for his products, the slogan 'Health without Medicine' soon had a thriving business. Although Allinson died in 1918, his sons succeeded him, and the company developed and soon owned mills across the country, from Wales to Yorkshire. Its Castleford Mill is still said to be the largest stone-grinding flourmill in the world.

A number of other companies sprang up on Allinson's coat tails, manufacturing brown bread for healthy eating, as Spiller's Turog, produced in Cardiff, which was, for a time, a major competitor of Hovis. This was marketed with such slogans as 'Keep Fit on Turog, bread of Health'.

But it was Hovis that grew to have the highest profile when it came to 'thinking brown'. Richard Smith, a miller in Macclesfield, believed in the health giving power of the wheat germ, and successfully researched how to separate it out, treat it, and return it to the mix, so that its health giving qualities were preserved, yet the resultant bread became longer lasting, obviously an additional desirable attribute. Tying up with a large-scale miller, Thomas Fitton, 'Smith's Patent Process Germ Flour' was launched in 1887. As a result of a competition an altogether

Above: Two posters from the 'Bread for energy' campaign, both issued by the Millers' Mutual Association and designed and produced by advertising agent Charles F. Higham, 1938.

more catchy name was adopted – Hovis – and in 1898 the company changed its name to The Hovis Bread Co. Ltd. (Hovis being derived from hominus vis – the strength of man). Although brown bread was confidently advertised as health giving, it was not actually until the mid-1920s that Allinson's and Smith's hunches were validated with the discovery of Vitamin D in wheat germ.

Bread advertising was all about 'strength' and 'energy'. When across-industry advertising was put out by the Millers' Mutual Association, using Charles Higham's advertising agency in the 1930s, it had service men striding out energetically and women athletes bestriding hurdles, accompanied by such tags as 'Get fit, keep fit, Bread for Energy'; bread became synonymous with the 'staff of life'. When brown bread advertising is mentioned, even

today, people start humming Dvorak's 'New World' symphony and Ridley Scott's 1973 Hovis television iconic advertisement immediately comes to mind with its image of a small boy pushing his bike up a cobbled Northern street. No press advertisement for bread, either before or since, can be judged to have had anything like the same impact.

Hovis was probably the most prolific advertiser of brown bread, often using classy magazines as the *Illustrated London News* or *Punch*. At the same time it was keeping its name ever before the public on the side of delivery vans, on permanent shop signs, with point of sale advertising, in recipe books, and, of course, on the side of its loaves themselves. Although the early Hovis advertising contained much copy explaining its benefits as an aid to digestion and as an energy giver, eventually it became so well known

that merely just an image of the loaf itself, or of full-of-life children, was found sufficient, with brief patriotic slogans as 'ensures a healthy race' or 'makes a fitter Britain', and, of course, dozens of variations on the theme 'Don't say brown, say Hovis'.

Press advertising, whether for Hovis or for other brands of bread, rarely achieved mention in the commercial art press for distinction of design. Apart from early Hovis advertisements, such as those produced by Mabel Lucie Atwell and Heath Robinson, the artists and graphic designers remain largely anonymous. Even the Millers' Mutual Association advertisements, initialed C.F.H., acknowledged the advertising agency rather than the artist.

Left: Press advertisement for the 'Bread for energy' campaign, Charles F. Higham, *Home Notes*, 1939.

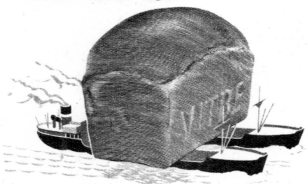

We've much to be thankful for

in this fourth year of War ... you can still get

FULL O' VITAMIN 'B'

VitBe

BROWN BREAD

FOR THE EXTRA VITAMIN 'B' YOU NEED

Left: VitBe Brown Bread press advertisement, *Picture Post*, March 1943.
Above: 'Turog – brown bread at its best' advertisement, Dorrit Dekk, *c.*1959.

EAT HOVIS

and do with a slice less !

BEST BAKERS BAKE IT *Macclesfield*

Above: 'Eat Hovis' advert, *Housewife*, January 1944. **Right:** 'Hovis: the better – balanced bread' press advertisement, *Housewife*, August 1948.

The breadwinner eats more Hovis now . . .

to keep up his strength the sensible way

Hovis THE BETTER-BALANCED BREAD

MILK
and milk substitutes

Milk and all that comes from milk...
increases melancholy.

Burton, 17th century

It is perhaps ironic that cows milk, which has been considered so essential for the upbringing of generations, has now been found not only to affect detrimentally lactose-intolerant people, but remedies are actually needed to combat this. Babies, however, seem immune, able to deal with the troublesome constituent, and, indeed milk, containing calcium, is key for the development of their bones and teeth, and its proteins and vitamins for growth in general.

A number of companies saw a niche market for mothers who were unable to breast feed and set about advertising the benefits of their various products to the extent that some of them became regularly sold in baby clinics subsidised by the government. The major players with such milk substitutes on sale in Britain were Nestlé's, 'Cow & Gate' and Glaxo's 'Ostermilk'. Nestlé's was of Swiss origin – a company formed in 1905 by an amalgamation of Henri Nestlé's condensed milk and infant formula milk company and that of the American brothers Charles and George Pane, the Anglo-Swiss Condensed Milk Company, both of which had been founded in the 1860s (Charles had been the U.S. Consul in Switzerland). Nestlé's early advertising of its baby milk made much of its Swiss roots –

From the milk of cows having an extensive range on the healthy and fertile sides of the Alps, breathing the Pure Air and feeding on the succulent grasses of the salubrious region.

Cow & Gate, on the other hand, stressed its Britishness. The brothers Charles and Leonard Gate,

Above: Poster by John Hassall for Nestlé's Swiss Milk, issued 1893. **Right:** Nestlé Malted Milk packaging label, undated.

from a family of Guilford grocers, decided to go into the dairy business and set up The West Surrey Central Dairy, selling its products in brown jugs with labels bearing the image of a cow looking over a gate, profiting from their surname. In 1900, they imported drying equipment from the States and, encouraged by the researches of one Dr. Killick Millard on the benefits of dried milk, Cow & Gate baby milk was first advertised in 1906. So successful was this that by the late 1920s the company adopted 'Cow & Gate' as its name. In 1930, Smiley, the baby with a crown on its head, was introduced into its advertising, with the slogan 'the food of royal babies', adding a touch of class to the Britishness of the product. This patriotic ring was continued in WWII with such tags as 'Children fed on Cow & Gate are growing up to build a saner, better world' – implying, without evidence, that its dry milk not only made children more physically healthy but more mentally wise!

Glaxo's origin was from a small general store in New Zealand, started by a Londoner, Joseph Nathan. The store added dairies and creameries to its operation and soon dried milk became one of its best-selling products. This they exported to England and sold as infant food under the brand

Nestlé's Malted Milk is pure cows' milk in powder form, to which cereals have been scientifically added. It is invigorating, very digestible and an excellent food for children, adults and invalids.

Nestlé's Malted Milk is a particularly refreshing drink for professional and business men, teachers, travelers, motorists and athletes, and is a delicious every day food for all the family.

NET WEIGHT 4¼ LBS.

NESTLÉ'S

REGISTERED — TRADE MARK

MALTED MILK

THIS BOTTLE CONTAINS A COMPOUND OF MILK AND EXTRACT OF MALTED BARLEY AND WHEAT

NESTLÉ AND ANGLO-SWISS CONDENSED MILK CO.

CHAM & VEVEY (SWITZERLAND) & LONDON

PREPARED IN U.S. AMERICA.

Flavoring — Nestlé's **Malted Milk** may be flavored by adding chocolate, vanilla, sugar, salt, nutmeg or flavoring extract.

Nestlé's Malted Milk is an ideal Baby Food. For directions and information see enclosed circular.

TO PREPARE

Use one to two tablespoonfuls of **Nestlé's Malted Milk** to a cup of water.

Mix thoroughly one-third cup of water and enough **Malted Milk** to form a thick paste. Fill the cup with either hot or cold water, stirring constantly. Do not use ice.

No. 2007

---

name Glaxo. Gradually the centre of gravity of the business shifted to London. In 1908 Glaxo was formally launched over here, boosted by the publication of the first Glaxo Baby Book, as 'the food that builds bonny babies'. By 1914 it had become a brand leader, sold through chemists and baby clinics. The company began to develop its research base, spurred on by the discovery of 'accessory food factors (vitamins), and was, in time, to become one of the major manufacturers of pharmaceuticals.

By 1928 it had added vitamins to its baby product, which it marketed generally as Sunshine Glaxo, but, in welfare centres, as Ostermilk. In 1932 Glaxo had both Ostermilk 1 and 2 on the market – 1 being sold as suitable for the first few months of life, and 2, a full cream product, for subsequent months. By WWII, the name Glaxo had been dropped for baby foods, to be replaced by Ostermilk.

Meanwhile milk was being marketed as a health-giving ingredient for diets for all ages. Two of the

Above: Glaxo press advertisement, *The Lady's Pictorial*, July 1924.
Right: 'Glaxo builds bonnie babies' press advertisement, *Punch*, 1932.
Far right: Nestlé's advertisement, illustrated by Frank Wiles, 1935.

major companies in the milk distribution business were United Dairies and Express Dairies. Express Dairies had been founded in 1864, when George Barham set up the Express County Milk Supply Company, with its main plant in Acton. It adopted the name 'Express', as its milk was distributed by train and it presumably hoped that this would conjure up the notion of 'speed', accompanied by 'freshness' to the minds of consumers. By the end of the century it had abbreviated its name to the Express Dairy Company and not only supplied milk but set up a chain of cafes throughout the country.

United Dairies was founded in 1917, a creamery, milk bottling and distribution company, an amalgamation of Wiltshire United Dairies, Metropolitan & Great Western Dairies and the Dairy Supply Company, who joined together as a united front with the aim of keeping afloat during WWI. It was United Dairies which, in 1920, pioneered pasteurized milk and pushed to ensure that children imbibed 'a quart a day'. By the 1950s it had become one of the largest concerns producing dairy products and, in 1959, absorbed Cow & Gate, the new company renamed Unigate.

Glaxo
WITH ADDED SUNSHINE VITAMIN 'D'

**Builds
Bonnie
Babies**

Glaxo is a balanced milk
food. It enables Baby
to develop completely
and naturally. Dense
bone . . . good teeth . . .
firm flesh . . . all are
equally assured.

GLAXO HOUSE,
56, OSNABURGH ST.
LONDON, N.W.1

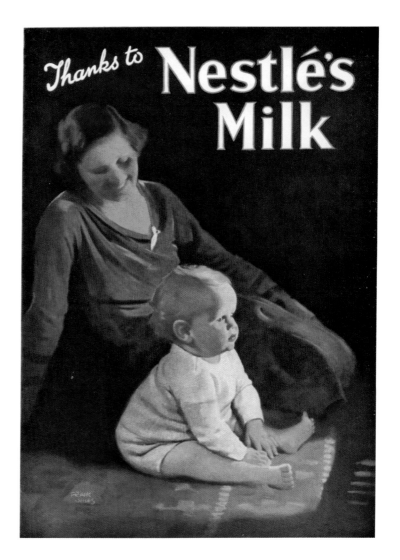

Thanks to **Nestlé's Milk**

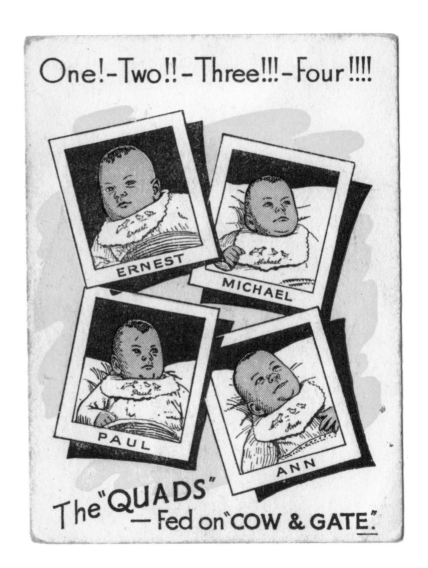

Above and right: Cow & Gate publicity,
'The Quads' collection cards, *c.*1930s.

HERE'S TO YOUR HEALTH

Window bill for United Dairies, by Muriel Dawson, Clowes Advertising Agency, 1932.

'Drink milk daily' poster, issued by the Milk Marketing Board, Ashley Havinden, 1936.

Milk THE FOOD OF FITNESS!

¶ "From the health standpoint there is no other single measure which would do more to improve the health, development and resistance to disease of the rising generation than a largely increased consumption of safe milk."

¶ "We attach such importance to milk that we prepared a special memorandum ... setting forth its value as a food."

¶ "Milk is of such outstanding value that the consumption of a sufficient quantity of it may be regarded as the key to proper nutrition."

Extracts from the First Report of
THE MINISTRY OF HEALTH ADVISORY COMMITTEE ON NUTRITION

DRINK AT LEAST A PINT A DAY!

Keep fit on Milk

You'll feel fighting fit if you drink more Milk

When it came to the advertising of milk as a health benefit the sea change came with the setting up of the Milk Marketing Board in 1933. There had previously been a National Milk Publicity Council established in 1922 to control milk production and distribution in an attempt to guarantee a minimum price to protect dairy farmers. This was to be relaunched in 1933, the Board's pre-war advertising was handled by Crawford's, and, in the immediate post-WWII years by Crawford's, Colman Prentis Varley, Mather & Crowther and Spearhead Services

Above left: 'Milk – the food of fitness' advert, 1937.
Above centre: 'Keep fit on milk' advert, 1937.
Above right: 'You'll feel fighting fit if you drink more milk' advert, 1957.

Ltd. 'Health' was very much the banner for milk campaigns albeit the main concern was economic.

Crawford's Art Director, Ashley Havinden, felt that he would have to come up with something exciting as 'everybody knew that people drank milk'. His radical solution was to have typography dominate the advertisements, dramatic typography placed diagonally – 'Drink Milk Daily' – nothing more. This was eventually to morph into Patrick Tilley's 'Drinka Pinta Milka Day', and, with a similar memorable rhythm 'milk's gotta lotta bottle'. And in the post-war years from 1954, when the Board was reconstituted, it resorted to using a young actress/model for much of its advertising, one Zoe Newton. *Art & Industry* complained –

…there is hardly an aspect of the milk story which can have been overlooked or any medium which has not been used.

None of this advertising felt it necessary to explain exactly how drinking milk could benefit health, but, by continual repetition on posters, in the press, on delivery vans etc. everyone took it to be so.

THE CHILD HE HADN'T SEEN

Leave at last ! Father is home again and this time, not only his wife but their child — their first — whom he's never seen, greet him with out-stretched arms.

How proud he is ! Snapshots after all don't tell one much, but here's the finest and best baby in the world.

When natural feeding failed the doctor advised mother to get Cow & Gate Milk Food, and baby from that day never looked back !

Why not get Cow & Gate for your Baby today, and also have the pleasure of seeing the look of pride on your husband's face when on his return home he sees what your loving care and Cow & Gate have together achieved !   ©3490

COW & GATE MILK FOOD *"Babies Love it!"*

Speak up for your Baby

Under the latest milk food regulations you may arrange, if you wish, to be left free to buy from your chemist or welfare centre the brand of milk that best suits your baby. All you do is to ask at the Food Office to have your baby's ration book *endorsed* to give you that freedom.

Baby's progress will tell you

OSTERMILK
is right

Ostermilk from Chemists costs 2/6 a 16 oz. tin. Send 3d. for the Ostermilk Baby Book to GLAXO LABORATORIES LTD. DEPT. 116, GREENFORD, MIDDLESEX

Above left: Cow & Gate advert, *Housewife*, July 1945.
Above right: Ostermilk advert, *Housewife*, August 1948.

DRINKS

A variety of drinks, usually taken hot, and more often drunk in the evening, came on to the market at the turn of the century, promising 'a good night's sleep', and sometimes suggesting that they could aid an extraordinary range of ailments from an unhealthy skin, to gastric ulcers, diabetes, and even cancer. These were largely made up from combinations and permutations of malt, wheat, whey, eggs, cocoa and natural sugars.

Horlicks was launched in America in 1883, by two brothers from Gloucestershire – James and William Horlick. It was initially intended as a baby food, but it was soon found more profitable to extend its suitability to all ages. James returned to England, and, by 1909, had set up a factory in Slough. His sons were to carry on the business and extend it across the world. The early advertising of Horlicks was handled by the Paul E. Derrick agency and was hyped both as a cold invigorating drink as well as a night time one 'smoothing excited nerves and bringing rejuvenating sleep'. It was not until 1931 that the term 'night starvation' was introduced. No one, including the manufacturer, quite understood how the product achieved what it claimed, but as it was later found to include useful vitamins and minerals it came to be appreciated as a generally beneficial and pleasant drink.

Ovaltine seems to have had a similar history. Developed in Switzerland, it was originally named Ovomaltine, egg and malt being its main ingredients. Story has it that it morphed into Ovaltine through some clerical error in translation. By 1909 it was being exported to England, and the market proved such as to warrant a factory being built in Kings

HORLICK'S GIVES YOU SOUND SLEEP
and INCREASES ENERGY by $\frac{1^{rd}}{3}$

SOUND, restful sleep! It's the first necessity to health and well-being—and here's the way to get it — drink a cupful of Horlick's hot — at bedtime. You will find that Horlick's soothes and warms your whole system, helps it to relax, calms jaded overstrung nerves. Soon you feel a pleasant drowsiness . . . Calm and relaxed, you sleep — deeply, *soundly* — as you should. While you are asleep the full nutriment in Horlick's repairs the wear and tear of the day so that (1) You wake refreshed. (2) Your energy is replaced. (3) Tests show Horlick's users have ⅓rd EXTRA energy at their command.

RESTLESS SLEEP — NO ENERGY NEXT DAY

NIGHTS passed like this have one result—they leave you *still tired*—unfit for work. Now — to-night, let Horlick's bring you sound sleep — then let its full nutriment build up energy — create EXTRA stores of it!

You can get Horlick's at Chemists and Stores in 4 sizes from 2/-. Made in England. The milk is in Horlick's — you need add water only.

Above: Horlicks advert, *Punch*, March 1933.
Right: Horlicks advert, *Picture Post*, April 1943.
Opposite left: Horlicks advert, 1931. **Opposite right:** Publicity for Ovaltine, 1929.

Please leave Horlicks for those who need it most

ONE REASON why Horlicks is scarce is that it is included in emergency rations supplied to sailors and airmen, who may have to live for many days without normal supplies of food.

Horlicks also goes to hospitals, to certain war factories, and to miners who are doing vital work under most trying conditions.

Nevertheless, some Horlicks is still being supplied to the shops. Please leave it for those who need it most. And make Horlicks by mixing it with water only. The milk is already in it.

HORLICKS

Langley. Ovaltine, as Horlicks, was to be variously advertised to be drunk hot or cold, and similarly became associated with 'a good night's sleep'; and again it was said to 'soothe the nerves' and 'rebuild energy and fitness for a new day'. In an attempt to distinguish itself from similar products such as Horlicks, Bourn-vita and Allenbury's Diet, its advertising sometimes suggested that it contained a mysterious mix of ingredients, which although never detailed, were nevertheless 'scientifically validated'.

Bovril, a meat rather than malt based drink, has been one of the longest best selling remedy,

vaguely advertised as a 'warm and warming drink'. By 1874, John Lawson Johnston, a Scotsman, was manufacturing Johnston's Fluid Beef in Canada. He returned to Britain in 1884, after his factory had burnt down, and started manufacturing again, his product now to be sold with the name Bovril (Bo = ox and Vril a word Johnston had come across in a novel meaning 'life force').

S.H. Benson, an ex-Royal Navy officer, joined Bovril in the early 1880s and, on leaving the company, established himself as an advertising agent in Fleet Street in 1893, taking Bovril as his

first client. It is generally acknowledged that Bovril's rapid expansion owed much to Benson's energy and originality. The Benson agency was to continue to provide Bovril's advertising through the whole period covered by this book.

Although the early advertisements were crammed with copy carrying recommendations from doctors and 'names', as that of Shackleton, it soon resorted to short catchy slogans. An early one was 'Alas my poor brother...', illustrated by W.H. Caffyn, showing a bull looking down on his smaller younger brother,

implying the meatiness of the product. But the slogan that most directly linked Bovril with health was 'Bovril prevents that sinking feeling', with images draw by H.H. Harris. This was used repeatedly, in a variety of ways, from the 1920s through to the 1950s. What 'that sinking feeling' was, and how Bovril prevented it, was never found necessary to be spelt out. A later series of advertisements, equally vague, linked Bovril with 'strength' by such slogans as 'Bovril puts beef into you', illustrated by Will Owen. Due to restrictions Bovril put out no advertisements during

Ovaltine MIXED Cold
is Delicious-Refreshing-Energising

The Best Summer Drink yet!

'OVALTINE' mixed Cold provides everything you could desire in a summer drink. It is deliciously creamy, coolly refreshing, revitalising and restorative. In fact it possesses all those exceptional health-giving qualities which have made 'Ovaltine' the world's most popular food beverage.

For this reason Cold 'Ovaltine' is an ideal supplement to light summer meals. It provides the important nutritive elements required to build up strength, energy and the necessary vitality for fitness. 'Ovaltine' Cold is easily prepared by adding 'Ovaltine' to cold milk, milk and water, or water only and mixing thoroughly.

P594A

Is last night's BOURN-VITA *helping you now?*

Are you getting every day the benefit of Bourn-vita? This delicious combination of British malt, new-laid eggs, full-cream milk and finest chocolate is a concentration of Nature's best waste-repairing and energy foods. The malt used in Bourn-vita is specially selected for its richness in diastase—a natural digestive. Thus this tonic-food not only supplies valuable nourishment but enables you to extract every ounce of nourishment from your other food. Start a course of Bourn-vita to-night and you will enjoy better sleep and wake up full of vigour.

Cadbury's BOURN-VITA

½ LB. WEIGHT GUARANTEED

FOR DIGESTION, SLEEP & ENERGY

Opposite left: 'Builds-up brain, nerve and body', Ovaltine advert, *Punch*, June 1930. **Opposite centre:** 'The best summer drink yet', Ovaltine advert, *Punch*, August 1939. **Opposite right:** Ovaltine advert, *Strand*, June 1949.

Above left: 'Ovaltine is delicious-refreshing-energising' advert, undated. **Above:** Cadbury's Bourn-vita advert, *Punch*, October 1935.

Ugh! – It's lucky I'm still 'WINTER-PROOFED'

Bedtime PROTECTIVE FOOD
*guards your health
this treacherous weather*

THANK goodness the shopping's done—it's a beast of a day. The sort of day when you're glad of the winter-proofing you get from *Bourn-vita*, with its four protective foods. Protective foods are needed this treacherous weather—they guard against the illness and infection that Spring and changeable weather always bring with them.

Down come the raindrops like dead larks dropping without songs—the pavement's wet and sloppy and your hat-brim drips down the back of your neck. Winter's just about over —or so the calendar says—but you still need *winterproofing*. You still need Bourn-vita's four protective foods to guard your health—its soothing power to give you deep restoring sleep.

You will be the better for *Bourn-vita*—make sure you have some for to-night.

Cadbury's

BOURN-VITA

9D
per ½ lb.
full weight

The **PROTECTIVE FOOD** *you drink at bedtime*

THE MORE YOU WORK-

the better sleep you need

You're not doing your bit if you're not really fit!

Here are two 'scientific sleep' tips to try out to-night. See how much better they make you feel in the morning!

1 Whatever your worries—*think of something that makes you feel happy for at least half-an-hour before bedtime every night*. Troubled sleep is unhealthy sleep.

2 Make a 'nightcup' of Bourn-vita a regular habit—it will soothe you, help digestion and calm your whole body.

Start taking these two hints to-night—and you'll find they make a world of difference to your pep and go.

With CADBURYS

BOURN-VITA

you'll be equal to it!

Still 1'5 per ½ lb

Above: Bourn-vita advert, Charles 'Clixby' Watson, 1937.
Right: 'The more you work – the better sleep you need' advert, *Housewife*, January 1944.

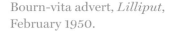

WWII after 1942, but after the war Little Bovril came
on the scene, a fetching little calf, accompanied by
the to be long lasting tag 'A Little Bovril goes a long
way'. Towards the end of the period of this book,
Bovril cashed in on the slimming mania with 'Fitness
without fatness'. The '50s also brought in its 'Glow'
campaign, with adults and children, with warmth
radiating from their bodies, on the way to work and
to school, illustrating what Bovril had been all about
in the first place – combatting the cold and colds.

Oxo, another meat extract product, was
manufactured from the 1860s, by the Liebig Extract
of Meat Company. Oxo in cube form was introduced
in 1910. Yet once more, its beneficial effects were
merely hinted. In 1908 it is recorded as being used
by Olympic athletes to 'fortify' them. In WWI it was
claimed that a soldier lost in No Man's Land survived
for a week solely on the unique, but unspecified,
qualities that Oxo contained. The 1930s brought in
the idea that it was 'refreshing'; and during WWII

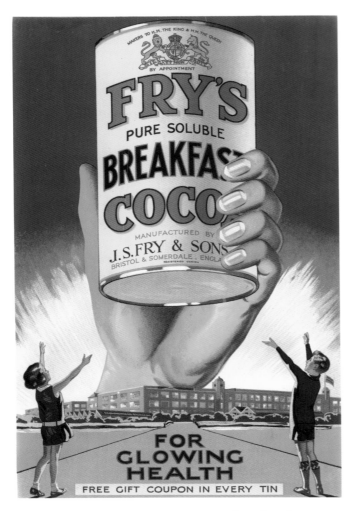

Fry's pure breakfast cocoa, display card, undated.

Bovril poster, Herbert H. Harris, 1920.

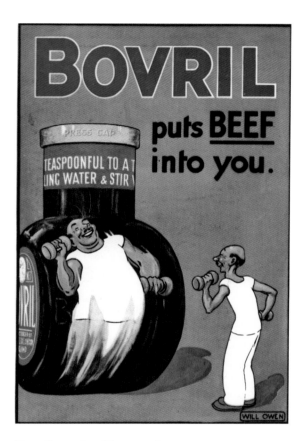

'Bovril puts beef into you' poster,
Will Owen, 1926.

'Glow to school with Bovril' poster, S.H. Benson Agency, 1951.

This is Dad going to the office he always drinks OXO at the office about elevensish he said OXO makes him work hard all day *Pam*

OXO *Prepared from PRIME RICH BEEF*

Above left: Oxo poster, undated. **Above right:** Oxo press advertisement, undated. **Right:** 'Goodnight children – everywhere' Oxo advert, *Punch*, July 1944. **Far right:** Oxo press advertisement, undated.

it was sold as 'a comforting drink in the shelter'. Its most familiar slogan 'Oxo works wonders' seems to have first appeared in the 1940s.

Other health-giving drinks relied on the word 'tonic', to imply that drinking them would give general well-being, sometimes the word 'wine' being added to suggest that drinking them would be fun as well as remedial. It was the Spaniards who first used quinine as a remedy for malaria; then followed French scientists, who, in the early nineteenth century, developed a compound containing quinine, which was manufactured and sold specifically to combat malaria. Tonic water was to contain quinine, but was advertised as a general 'pick-me-up', with the amount of quinine being reduced over the years so that it eventually became more of a social, than a medicinal, drink. The word 'tonic' tended to be retained, as with Schweppes Tonic Water, whose product was advertised with Barabal's images of beautiful women in the 1920s and '30s, the 'does you good' whimsies from the agency Winter Thomas in the '30s, to be followed by George Him's and Stephen

"*Goodnight children — everywhere*"

Never still for a moment. What energy they use! Now's the time for that long refreshing sleep — a cup of OXO and off to bed.

OXO

Prepared from **PRIME RICH BEEF**

A Really Popular

AND REFRESHING BEVERAGE

FOR CUP AND COOKING

OXO CUBE BRAND

MAKES PERFECT GRAVY

A comfort in the Shelter

FRESH AND VIGOROUS

NO NERVINESS & NO NEURALGIA

Miss Joyce Barbour, one of the Daintiest of our leading Revue Artistes, who is at present playing in "Mayfair to Montmartre," at the New Oxford Theatre, London, W., writes :—" For the last few years I have been almost continuously playing in revue, in which one is called upon to act, sing and dance alike with equal facility. In conjunction with rehearsals, this would, of course, be an unending and unendurable strain ; but fortunately I have been able to rely upon Phosferine for all the extra energy I need, and, as I am always able to enjoy my work, the fact speaks for itself. Certainly, since I have had recourse to Phosferine I feel that I work or play at my best, and nowadays am never troubled with ' nerviness,' neuralgia, or, in fact, any kind of nerve disorders or overstrain, for which happy conditions I am convinced Phosferine is entirely responsible, as I always feel fresh and vigorous enough to fulfil whatever is expected of me."

PHOSFERINE
CURES AND PREVENTS
NERVE WEAKNESS
AND RE-VITALISES THE WHOLE NERVE SYSTEM
The Greatest of all Tonics
A PROVEN REMEDY FOR

Influenza	Neuralgia	Lassitude	Rheumatism
Indigestion	Maternity Weakness	Neuritis	Malaria
Sleeplessness	Premature Decay	Faintness	Headache
Exhaustion	Mental Exhaustion	Brain-Fag	Nerve Shock
Nervous Debility	Loss of Appetite	Anæmia	Sciatica

Liquid and Tablets. The 3/- size contains nearly four times the 1/3 size.

Potter's Schweppshire fancies in the 1950s and '60s.

Although Schweppes Tonic Water is, perhaps, best known, there were a number of other tonic waters and wines on the market at the same time, regularly marketed as 'remedial' – Hall's Wine 'that strengthens you', Phospherine 'that keeps you absolutely fit' and 'banishes depression', Sanatogen 'you can feel it does you good' and Buckfast Tonic Wine, sold with the tag 'three small glasses a day for good health and lively blood'. Wincarnis, which was originally a Liebig product, was produced in England from the 1880s by Coleman & Co. of Norwich. A typical advertisement in the 1920s has blithe spirits, in silhouette, dancing around a bottle of the brew, with, in large type, 'A Good Tonic Wine'; whilst another, from the same period, illustrated by the then celebrated Septimus Scott, had the same wording, accompanied by a conquering Viking, presumably implying his body stoked by Wincarnis.

But by far the most prolifically and amusingly advertised drink claiming to be 'healthy' was Guinness, the company sticking loyally to the same advertising agency, S.H. Benson's, for some forty years. Although Arthur Guinness set up a small brewery as early as 1759, it is not really until the

A Jugoslav poet called Peter
Wrote odes without sense, rhyme or metre,
Till he turned from Slavonic
Despair to Schweppes Tonic
And verses like this one but neater.

Schweppes
TONIC WATER
- does you Good

Left: Press advertisement for Phosferine tonic, undated. **Above:** 'Schweppes tonic water – does you good' press advert, *Punch*, October 1935. **Right:** Guinness, Penguinness advert, Ronald Searle, undated.

OUTPOSTS OF GUINNESS

Penguinness

From an article by a member of Sir Douglas Mawson's Antarctic expedition of 1929.

" *The stores* " *(left by Mawson's earlier expedition of 1911)* " *were in good condition after 18 years : cocoa, salt, flour and matches from these stores were actually used afterwards . . . There were also four bottles of Guinness on a shelf, which, although frozen, were put to excellent use."*

The Belfast Telegraph, April 10th, 1933.

The goodness of Guinness is un-affected by climate. Wherever you drink it, in frozen north or sunny south, it always comes to you in the prime of condition.

GUINNESS
IS GOOD FOR YOU

I wood if I could...

I wish that I could bowl a wood
To any length required,
And keep it up till sun goes down,
Without my getting tired.

But for a length, you need the strength
To put behind your wood,
Could Guinness do that trick for me?
My woodness . . . yes it good!

G.E.1310.B

'I wood if I could...', Guinness advert, S.H. Benson
Agency, c.1942.

Have a glass of Guinness when you're Tired

G.E.677

'Have a glass of Guinness when you're tired' advert,
Jim Bateman, 1946.

Heroes are good for a cheering,
Villains are good for a boo,
Heroines good for a leering,
And **GUINNESS** is good for **YOU**

G.E.4197·B

twentieth century that drinking Guinness became blatantly linked to health. Until the 1920s its advertising was relatively low key, only occasionally containing a doctor's recommendation or some such; but in the 1920s Guinness, competing as it was with tied houses, decided to review its advertising and began to mount strong campaigns, albeit the rather cautious management made the proviso that these 'should be done well and in good taste'. It was Oswald Greene, a Director of Benson's, who produced the slogan 'Guinness is good for you'; and, with the appointment of Martin Pick (brother of Frank Pick of London Underground) as Guinness's advertising manager, the first of these campaigns was launched in 1929. Greene thought up seven reasons why Guinness 'was good for you' and these included such fancies as 'rebuilding brain cells'. Soon such specifics were found to be unnecessary – everybody came to accept that Guinness was good for you – and when John Gilroy was used by Benson's and injected his humour, 'strength' was added to the many benefits of the drink. Gilroy was to work on these campaigns for some thirty years, designing to such familiar slogans as 'My goodness, My Guinness', and introducing his menagerie of animals. The Company

resorted to a vast number of publicity ruses over the years of which their spoofs of Alice in Wonderland are, perhaps, now the most valued by collectors of ephemera. In 1936, the American Federal Alcohol Administration unsuccessfully challenged the health claims of the product, and so Guinness has been allowed to remain 'Good for us', at least its advertisements making us happy, if our bodies were not remarkably affected one way or another.

HYGIENE

Good health and longevity depends much on personal cleanliness and a variety of habits and customs or minute attentions ... when combined there is every reason to believe that much additional health and comfort would arise from their observance.

Virginia Smith, 2008

Virginia Smith in her erudite book *Clean*, has hygiene as a basic protective instinct, linking it to animal grooming. The actual form of human beings' disgust at dirt and bad odours, and delight in cleanliness and sweet smells, are, however, culturally determined, even with individual differences within any one culture. Although the very derivative of the word 'hygiene' is 'health', and, perhaps therefore there has always been a glimmer of a link between the two, the actual mechanism of this link only came from the very steep learning curve in the medical, pharmaceutical and biological sciences in the nineteenth century, along with the deeds and words of such urban sanitary reformers as John Snow, Edwin Chadwick and Joseph Bazalgette. By the end of the century householders would have become aware of the danger of dirt, and had to begin to learn to discriminate between the plethora of products coming on to the market to 'fight' germs and bacteria, for much of the language hyping the different products resorted to battle terminology.

Early liquids to combat germs, which were to become market leaders were Izal, introduced by Newton Chambers in 1893, and John Jeye's Jeyes Fluid, receiving its Royal Warrant in 1896; Milton was introduced by the Milton Pharmaceutical Co.

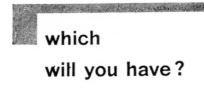

which will you have?

MILTON or FLU

you can't have both!

MILTON Antiseptic

Previous page: 'Vim – a child can use it' advert, Will Owen, 1920s.

in 1916, said to be so called as it was produced in the house where Milton had lived; and TCP, first manufactured in 1918 (the initials derived from its lengthy chemical name). Harpic, devised by Harry Pickup in Scarborough, did not appear until the 1920s, and Dettol not until the 1930s. Dettol, one of the most commercially successful, later was sold in a variety of forms, such as soap, cream and plasters. Harpic was mainly used for toilets, whereas the others were offered as having more general cleansing uses.

The challenge for manufacturers of disinfectants was how to produce something that would kill germs, yet be otherwise harmless. Many products had their early testing in hospitals for disinfecting skin during operations, and made much of this in their advertising, particularly during WWII. Dettol, Milton and TCP stressed their efficacy for grazes, stings, spots and pimples, and general personal hygiene. TCP became additionally sold as a mouthwash, and Milton for sterilizing babies bottles, cashing in on its successful use in a severe outbreak of infant gastroenteritis in the 1940s. All three claimed distinction for their specific smells and colours, Dettol changing miraculously

Well played—but played out!

Pores to consider—

have an

IZAL BATH

Izal 1/9 a bottle

LET ENERGY IN — THROUGH THE PORES OF THE SKIN

After the match run a hot bath, add a few shakes of IZAL antiseptic, jump in and simmer gently for 20 minutes • Spring out, with pores stimulated, overheated blood cooled and fatigue drained away with the dirty water. Whenever you're deadbeat, come back in an IZAL bath.

Warm classrooms,
chilly playgrounds, and
plenty of colds about . . .

A sensible mother starts their
day with a MILTON gargle

"Tell me, doctor . . . You say that

blood-poisoning is caused by germs—no matter how clean the cut may seem to be. How am I to protect myself? Is there an efficient, non-poisonous antiseptic I can safely apply direct to a cut or injury?"

The way to prevent blood-poisoning is to get rid of the germs which cause it. 'Dettol' — the modern antiseptic — kills germs. On body tissues it is bland, non-poisonous, non-corrosive, non-staining. It is clean and clear and pleasant in smell — yet three times more effective germicidally than pure carbolic acid.

Whenever you cut or scratch yourself, apply 'Dettol' freely and fearlessly (*see directions*). A break in the skin is a wide-open door to the germs of septic infection. Keep 'Dettol' handy — use it in time.

Use 'Dettol' promptly in time of accident
Your Chemist has it — in bottles 1/- and 3/-

'DETTOL' THE MODERN ANTISEPTIC

TRADE MARK

RECKITT AND SONS LIMITED (PHARMACEUTICAL DEPT.), LONDON AND HULL

Picture Post, July 1, 1939

"Tell me, doctor . . .

I can't very well keep the children from the risk of all infection at school . .

. . . . but isn't there any simple precaution we could take when they come home?" One of the simple and sensible precautions against the risk of infection which we can all take is this — simply add some 'Dettol' to the evening bath, just before bed.

The antiseptic distinguished by the brand name 'Dettol' is absolutely non-poisonous and non-staining. It is as ruthless to germs as it is gentle to human tissue. Added to the bath it disinfects and cleanses the smallest break in the skin which even the child itself may not have noticed. Owing to its pleasant smell and tonic action it is so refreshing that children will easily consider it a daily treat.

"*. . . highly infectious of course: but the doctor told us always to add some 'Dettol' to the wash basin, and no one else caught it.*"

'DETTOL' TRADE MARK

THE MODERN ANTISEPTIC

Your chemist sells 'Dettol' in bottles 1/-, 1/9 and 3/-

RECKITT & SONS, HULL & LONDON. (PHARMACEUTICAL DEPT., HULL)

AIR RAID

PRECAUTIONS

Be prepared for any emergency and keep 'DETTOL', the modern antiseptic, in your First Aid kit.

'Dettol' is your protection against infection. Take action now! Go to your chemist and buy a bottle.

1/-, 1/9 and **3/-** bottles.

'DETTOL' TRADE MARK

THE MODERN ANTISEPTIC
Non-poisonous

RECKITT AND SONS, HULL AND LONDON
(PHARMACEUTICAL DEPT., HULL)

from reddish gold to white when water was added. Dettol's advertising was typical for such products with slogans as 'be 100% sure' and 'protector from germs', with a battle trademark of a sword. A 1950s Dettol advertisement listed reasons why it was the product to buy – killer of germs, non-toxic, safe, stable, persistent, non-corrosive, doesn't stain, gentle, painless for open wounds, and effective in the presence of blood.

Disinfectant in soap rather than liquid form had actually arrived earlier on the scene. Mr. Wright's Coal Tar Soap (using carbolic acid, a derivative from coal tar) was manufactured by Mr. Wright in Southwark, coming to the market in 1866, and selling itself as a 'protection from infection'. This was about the same time as Lister was working with carbolic acid as a possible disinfectant in hospitals, but the company history makes no mention of this.

Wright's soap, as so many other products, benefited from its use by troops in wartime, as in a WWI advertisement, which has a soldier writing to thank his girl friend for the soap she had sent in her parcel to the front – 'It's grand stuff that makes you feel absolutely fit'.

Far left: Dettol advert, *Picture Post*, 1939.
Left: 'The Modern Antiseptic', Dettol, 1939.
Above: TCP advert, *Picture Post*, April 1943.

It was not until some thirty years after the introduction of Wright's Coal Tar Soap, in 1894, that Lever Bros. began to produce a similar product, marketed as Lifebuoy, but sold only as a household disinfectant for washing linen and cleaning surfaces. It did not take its toilet bar form, for personal hygiene, until 1933, with the additional benefit added of it acting as a deodorant. Early advertising for Lifebuoy featured a seaman with a lifebelt, along with variations of the slogans 'Lifebuoy saves lives', and 'Join the Lifebuoy Crusade'. By the late '20s the seaman made fewer appearances and the message became blunt – 'Lifebuoy for Health'.

Lever Bros. already had a household soap on the market, introducing Sunlight in 1884, but this was based on glycerin and vegetable oils and had the advantage of smelling of lemons (albeit many remember nostalgically the pungent smell of Wright's Coal Tar and Lifebuoy).

Sunlight was the first soap to be sold cut up and in wrapped bars and impressed as a shade more classy than Lifebuoy, attracting a Royal Warrant. By 1920, Lever Bros. had acquired Pear's soap (emanating from Andrew Pear's Soho barber shop

Far left: Wright's Coal Tar Soap, *The Sketch*, March 1922. **Left:** Bookmark for Wright's Coal Tar Soap, undated. **Above:** Wright's Coal Tar advert, *c.*1917.

in 1807), but this was always marketed as cosmetic, albeit the word 'clean' sometimes appeared in its advertisements. As with the disinfectants, the soaps sold as for hygiene rather than cosmetic benefits, and used military analogies – they were fighting a constant battle against dirt and germs.

LIFEBUOY in the home gives health protection to the family

Three generations of mothers have relied upon the antiseptic lather of

LIFEBUOY

to wash away the germs in dirt.

2½d per 4-oz. tablet — 1 coupon
(nett weight when manufactured)

'Lifebuoy in the home gives health protection to the family' press advertisement, *Houswife*, January 1944.

Skin health the foundation of beauty

Mother— the health doctor

Mothers know dirt for what it is—and fear it.

They will not tolerate dirty schools, dirty streets, dirty homes or dirty children.

Lifebuoy Soap is one of the most widely used soaps in the world because mothers appreciate its scientific protection against the dangers of dirt

Mothers know that Lifebuoy lather goes down deep into every pore, and removes impurities. They know that Lifebuoy keeps the skin soft, pliable, and glowing with health—that it is bland, pure and soothing to the tenderest skin—even that of a baby.

Buy Lifebuoy in the new pack, two large cakes in a carton.

Lifebuoy Soap
for HEALTH

THEY are daughters to be proud of—those quickly-growing, energetic girls. Their sparkling eyes, supple carriage, skins lovely with the clear flush of radiant health, are messages of cheer to the mothers who watch their development with anxious care. The vigorous outdoor sports of to-day, which have ousted the embroidery and sampler making of yesterday, mean health and beauty to girlhood. One sees few complexions of the hot-house type to-day. Exercise means skin health. Yet that healthiness is a challenge to the germs of disease and impurities that are ever waiting for a congenial resting place to work their mischief.

Guard their skin health

Mothers! See that these dangerous impurities do not work havoc with the fresh beauty of your girls' complexions. Guard their skin health, for it is in the pores of the skin that harmful germs find a lodging. See that their daily bath is taken with Lifebuoy Soap. Give them a tablet each week to keep in their school lockers. It will mean a clear, radiant skin when they attain womanhood.

Germs live in the pores

Put a cake of Lifebuoy at every place in your house where hands are washed, to be used by everybody—old and young. Dirt and impurities lodge in the pores of the skin. Ordinary cleansing doesn't remove them. The rich lather of Lifebuoy, with its wonderful health element, goes deep down into the pores and routs out the enemies of the skin. The healthy odour vanishes, but the protection remains. Get Lifebuoy now. Buy it in the *new pack*, two large cakes in each carton. Lever Brothers Limited, Port Sunlight.

Above: Lifebuoy press advert, *Punch*, January 1936.
Opposite: Advertising insert for Sunlight Soap, Bert Thomas, *c.*1910.

THIS HAPPENED TO ME

CLOTHING

The history of fashion provides numerous examples of clothes that were actually harmful to one's health, from tight corsets to stiletto heels, but the nineteenth century brought to the market two examples of clothes that were conceived from the start as health giving. Although both were developed from scientific, or rather pseudo-scientific ideas, Jaeger and Aertex actually took opposing stands – the former promoting wool and animal coverings as most beneficial to cover humans, the latter arguing the benefits of plant derived textiles.

In 1882, Dr. Gustav Jaeger put over his ideas on dress reform in his book *Health Culture*. A medical doctor, he had had a somewhat curious career running a zoo before entering academic life, initially as Professor of Zoology and Anthropology at Hohenheim Academy, and then as a lecturer at the Royal Polytechnic at Stuttgart.

The basis of Jaeger's theory on clothing was his observation that animals seemed generally healthier than humans, and appeared immune to the chills and colds that humans had when exposed to bad weather. This led him to believe that what covered animals should cover humans – that clothes derived from animal skins would be most beneficial, and, when tightly fitted to the body, would maintain an even temperature. He proposed a balance of wool fabric layering that would be enough to provide heat yet be airy enough to allow for perspiration. Jaeger considered that putrid air caused mental anxiety, but that moving air round the body could cure obesity, smallpox, scarlet fever, typhus and even rabies.

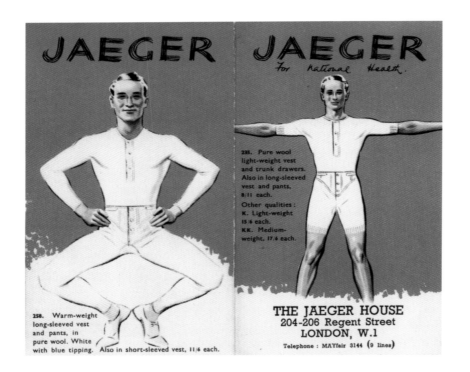

JAEGER

JAEGER
For National Health.

258. Warm-weight long-sleeved vest and pants, in pure wool. White with blue tipping. Also in short-sleeved vest, 11/6 each.

235. Pure wool light-weight vest and trunk drawers. Also in long-sleeved vest and pants, 8/11 each. Other qualities : K. Light-weight 15/6 each. KK. Medium-weight, 17/6 each.

THE JAEGER HOUSE
204-206 Regent Street
LONDON, W.1
Telephone : MAYfair 3144 (9 lines)

His suggested clothing, he considered, should be made up of preferably undyed wool and should be tightfitting, with fastenings at openings to prevent rushes of air; on these ideas he founded Dr. Jaeger's Woollen System & Co.

It was Lewis Tomalin who, inspired by Jaeger's theories, translated his book, and obtaining both his patents and the name, started manufacturing Jaeger clothes in 1884. Soon these were taken up by the great and the good, the likes of Bernard Shaw appearing in what became his signature clothing, a furry reddish brown suit a la Jaeger. Although Jaeger was not involved in the company, and died in 1917, Tomalin's company thrived, and underpinned the 'scientific' basis of its clothing by taking on an academic chemist specialising in textiles; A.E. Garrett became the spokesman for Jaeger's cause for many years, advocating the use of a range of animal

Left: 'Jaeger for National Health' booklet, 1944.
Right: Jaeger leaflet, c.1942. Below right: 'Jaeger
– the vogue in woollens' booklet, c.1929.

furs including sheep, cashmere, alpaca, vicuna and camel, the last becoming particularly connected with the name Jaeger.

Early Jaeger advertising made much of the health aspect, with such tags as 'Jaeger Pure Wool Prevents Chills', 'The Time to Wear Wool is all the Time' and 'Warm in winter, cool in summer'. Over the years, the remedial slant gradually faded away, but Jaeger clothes were to be always associated with stylish sportswear with their woolly bathing costumes at one time as fashionable as their camel hair coats. The company's image was enhanced by the modernistic architecture of its shops, and the jazziness of its advertising when Crawford's was brought in for its re-launching in the mid-1930s. Yet there were strands of its 'healthy' origins lingering into the 1940s and '50s, examples being a leaflet for women's clothing entitled 'Jaeger knitwear for Health, Quality and Comfort', and another for menswear headed 'Jaeger for National Health'.

'Aertex' was a brand that was as equally evangelical about plant-based textiles as Jaeger had been about animal based ones. At much the same time as Tomalin was exploiting Jaeger's theories, Lewis Haslam, a Lancashire mill owner, staying in

Aertex evens up temperatures

The British climate might well be compared to a joint of beef; hot, Monday — cold, Tuesday — and, only too often, hash, slush or what have you on Wednesday! But to the Aertex ventilated body temperatures just don't count. The unique cellular mesh is a true insulator that literally keeps you cool on warm days, warm on cold days and fresh and comfortable in the muggiest weather. There are Aertex blouses and underwear for ladies, and shirts, pyjamas and underwear of varying weights for men all on the same wonderful principle. Send for complete catalogue—and, when buying, always see the *Aertex* label.

Aertex linings keep you air-conditioned in **DUNLOP** *waterproofs*

a sanatorium for a spell, also became interested in the circulation of air around the body. He persuaded the owners of the sanatorium, Sir Benjamin Ward Richardson and Dr. Richard Greene, that clothing which trapped air near the skin could promote a healthy life-style. The two joined with Haslam in 1888, to manufacture clothes from a cotton fabric which trapped air between the warp and the weft. It was originally branded Cellular Clothing with the motto 'Ventus textilis – Calor Aequalis' (woven from air – even heat) but it was ruled that Cellular was a common word that could not be branded, and, by 1899, it had been renamed 'Aertex' – the name being derived from 'aerate' and 'textile'. Much was made, in its advertising, of the body now being better able to breathe being 'clothed in air', in contrast to wool that became clotted with sweat and did not allow for aeration.

As with Jaeger, Aertex was taken up by outdoor enthusiasts in the 1920s and '30s, and became standard wear for school and club sporting activities, perhaps never attaining, or even aiming to attain, the classiness of Jaeger; its image has always tended to be more workaday, albeit it was recently oddly featured in a Stella McCartney fashion show, a

There are many imitations

The continued popularity of Aertex cellular fabric over sixty years has led to many inferior imitations, often loosely described as "Aertex." But the *real* Aertex is unique. It has never been successfully copied. You can tell it by this label.

but only one
AERTEX

Genuine Aertex garments bear this label

THE CELLULAR CLOTHING CO LTD
AERTEX
LONDON

—and utility

CELLULAR CLOTHING CO
Aertil
THE LONDON CO LTD

AERTEX for

men's, women's and

kiddies' underwear,

shirts and pyjamas

The ingenious Aertex weave keeps the body at a healthful, even temperature in heat or cold. For year round comfort wear Aertex, so durable and so easy to wash.

See this label on all garments

AERTEX

When in LONDON visit Oliver Bros. Ltd., the AERTEX shop at 455, Oxford Street, W.1 who handle the personal export scheme, thus avoiding purchase tax. Just select what you want of "The world's most healthful wear" and the Aertex goods will be delivered straight to your ship or overseas address. If you cannot call we will gladly send you a catalogue.

lxxiv

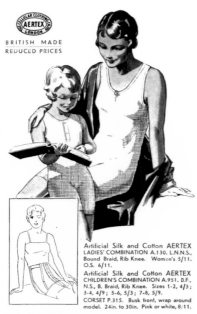

new style termed Sport Luxe! By WWII Aertex
clothing had become a standard part of British and
Commonwealth servicemen's kit and was considered
essential for clothing for the Women's Land Army.

Aertex retained 'healthiness' as its unique selling
point, right through the period of this book, typical
advertisement of 1953 declaring –

*In hot weather the thousands of tiny air-cells in
the Aertex cellular weave ventilate your body; yet
come a cold spell and they keep you cozily warm and
safe from chills.*

Left: Aertex advert, undated. **Right:** 'Pants with a
purpose' advert, *Punch*, April 1938. **Far right:** 'There is
no substitute for wool' press advert, *Milady*, June 1952.

Pants with a Purpose
—to keep you FIT
—even though you sit all day!

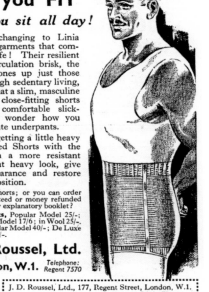

Men everywhere are changing to Linia Shorts, the modern undergarments that combat the evils of civilized life! Their resilient elastic weave keeps the circulation brisk, the intestines working well, tones up just those regions that get slack through sedentary living, and wards off fat. And what a slim, masculine trimness of figure these close-fitting shorts give! When you wear comfortable slick-fitting Linia Shorts, you wonder how you tolerated flapping, effeminate underpants.

Men whose figures are getting a little heavy prefer the Linia Reinforced Shorts with the abdominal part woven in a more resistant weave. These banish that heavy look, give youthful health and appearance and restore the abdominal organs to position.

Call in and see these Linia Shorts; or you can order by post. Perfect fitting guaranteed or money refunded in full. May we send you a fully explanatory booklet?

Prices per pair: **Linia Shorts,** Popular Model 25/-; De Luxe Model 50/-; Standard Model 17/6; in Wool 25/-. **Linia Reinforced Shorts:** Popular Model 40/-; De Luxe Model 63/-; Standard Model 25/-.

On Sale Only at J. Roussel, Ltd.
177 Regent St., London, W.1.
Telephone: Regent 7570

And at 43, Cheapside, E.C.2, and five other London branches. Branches also at **Birmingham:** 14, New St.; **Bournemouth:** Hampshire House; **Bristol:** 53, Park St.; **Edinburgh:** 1, Frederick Street; **Glasgow:** 345, Sauchiehall St.; **Hove:** 66, Western Rd.; **Leicester:** 1, Bishop Street; **Liverpool:** 6, South John St.; **Manchester:** 12, King St.; **Nottingham:** 25a, Milton St.; **Southport:** 114, Lord St.

SPAS AND SEASIDE RESORTS

But if one was something of a hypochondriac …
and stood in need of cures for a different number of complaints,
this could entail a progress of a nation-wide Odyssey..

Dr. Vernon Cole

Aside from the Roman baths in Bath, therapeutic centres in Britain are, by some authors, traced back to the holy wells with their associated saints, the goodness of the latter, as if by osmosis, imbuing the holiness of the former. Certainly by the late sixteenth and seventeenth centuries, Harrogate, Tonbridge, Epsom and Wells, all had discovered that they possessed 'healing' waters that could be exploited. By the eighteenth and early nineteenth centuries, these watering places had become as much known for their licentiousness as for their remedies, albeit the former could well have been more effective in dealing with melancholia and generally lifting people's spirits.

Each venue, in their turn, had their fashionable periods and their dips, but it was not really until the nineteenth century that spas became altogether more seriously focused on health rather than pleasure, with strict dietary regimes and an amazing variety of water treatments. Towards the end of the century spas became increasingly concerned to align themselves to the scientific discoveries of the time, and began to harness electricity and even radium for treatments, some offered as 'cure-alls' although most centred their 'expertise' on alleviating rheumatism, arthritis and gastric disorders.

As early as 1753, Dr. Charles Russell had published 'The Uses of Sea Water', and once George

Above: 'Harrogate – Britain's Health Resort' poster, 1910. **Right:** Advert for Spielplatz, private recreation grounds, St Albans.

III had dipped his toe into the sea at Weymouth, coastal towns began to join the 'spa' bonanza. At the time, there was no sound evidence as to the curative qualities of the treatments offered either by the inland or seaside spas – the sea dips, the mud baths, the electropathy, the compressed air-baths, the wet-sheeting and the like, all attracted criticism from medical orthodoxy. Of course keeping clean, swathed in wet sheets in a hydro, or braving the seas at Margate, would in itself have benefited one's health. In that many inland spas banned the really seriously ill, and in that there was no doubt a good deal of spontaneous recovery through sensible dieting and exercising, the spas were able to claim their various shenanigans to be effective remedies. In addition, there is always the placebo effect brought about by attention, at least civil, and oftimes unctuous, of the 'medical' staff employed.

By the 1920s many of the large hydro buildings had become private schools, inland spas had become mere pleasure resorts from which to view the picturesque countryside, and seaside towns had morphed into holiday venues. Nowadays the word 'spa' is grandiosely attached to any hostelry that besports a swimming pool and offers massages

MATLOCK

THE PEAK DISTRICT SPA AND HOLIDAY RESORT
"THE METROPOLIS OF HYDROPATHY"

SERVED BY
LMS MAIN LINE

WRITE PUBLICITY SECRETARY.
TOWN HALL, MATLOCK,
FOR FREE OFFICIAL GUIDE.

A.D 664

FLEETWOOD
FOR HEALTH & PLEASURE

ONWARD

and manicures. Nevertheless many towns clung on to their supposed health giving attributes well into the twentieth century, with relevant advertising to ensure that visitors appreciated this aspect of their holidays or day trips. A publicity booklet issued by Bath in 1924, illustrated by Charles Paine, had on its cover 'in the eighteenth century and today Bath the premier health and pleasure resort'; whilst a similar booklet for Great Yarmouth, in 1928, illustrated by Septimus Scott, invited visitors for 'happy healthy holidays'. Torquay, in a 1929 advertisement, listed forty treatments it could offer, including the Bourbon-Lacy bath and diathermy. Along with civic advertising there was a certain amount of advertising by specific establishments. One curious example was for the Spielplatz in St. Albans, which appeared regularly in the 'Health and Efficiency' magazine in the inter-war years, showing happy unclothed tennis players – 'Get health and joy through nudism'.

But some of the best spa and health resort advertising was that which appeared on the railways, often funded by financial tie-ups between various railway companies and towns on their routes. In the 1920s LMS advertised reduced fares to certain health resorts and boosted the health giving attractions of

Far left: LMS poster for Matlock, Henry Holder, 1920s. Left: 'Fleetwood for health & pleasure', official guide, 1949. Above: 'Hastings for Health' advert, *Picture Post*, July 1939.

Caledonian Railway poster for Droitwich, unsigned, 1910.

such towns as Droitwich Spa, with a poster designed by Leonard Cusden declaring it to have 'the greatest natural brine baths for treatments of rheumatism, sciatica, arthritis etc.', and for Blackpool selling it as a place where one could 'Get fit and keep fit'. Matlock was yet another destination that LMS hyped as 'The Metropolis of Hydropathy'. LNER did not lag far behind, having Harrogate on its line; whilst from the 1910s through to the 1950s GWR was showing off some of its own 'healthy' towns, as Llandrindod Wells – 'for healing springs, pure air and recreation', and Bournemouth 'for health and pleasure'; the 'innate releasing mechanism', as psychologists would term any trigger, being the word 'health'.

HERE'S TO YOUR HEALTH

TORQUAY
for SUNSHINE and SPA TREATMENTS

TORQUAY, with its splendid record of sunshine, its ultra-violet rays, and its warm western breezes, will do all that Nature can to make you well and happy. And those who need medical treatments to preserve or restore their health will find the Medical Baths perfectly equipped for every kind of treatment and cure. Torquay Medical Baths undoubtedly form one of the most up-to-date and luxurious modern spa establishments in Europe.

List of Spa Treatments available :

BALNEOLOGICAL.

Hot Sea Water, with Blanket Pack
Deep Bath
Seaweed Bath
Carbonic Acid Bath
Oxygen Bath
Vapour
Aix Douche-Massage
Vichy Douche-Massage
Pine Bath
Plombières (Intestinal Lavage)
Turkish Bath
Bourbon-Lancy Bath
Needle Spray
Sitz Douche
Scotch Douche
Sulphur Bath
Bran, Oatmeal or Soda Bath
Peat Bath and packs
Brine Bath (Concentrated Sea Water)
Contrast Bath
Salt Rub
Iodine Bath
Nauheim Bath

ELECTRICAL.

Bristow Coil
Two or Four Cell Schnee Bath
Dowsing Radiant Heat
Electric Heat "Sun" Cabinet
Cataphoresis (Ionic Medication)
Diathermy (Electro-Thermal Penetration)
Electro-Vibro Massage
Electro Massage
Faradism, Galvanism or Sinusoidal Currents
High-Frequency Current
Ultra-Violet Rays (Artificial Sunshine) (Carbon Arc or Mercury Vapour)

ACCESSORY.

Throat, Nose or Ear Irrigations
Liver Packs
Pistany Mud Packs
Dartmoor Peat Packs
Massage
Swedish Massage
Chiropody

NEW "VITA"-GLASS SUN LOUNGE – THE LARGEST IN THE BRITISH ISLES – OPEN EVERY DAY FOR ULTRA-VIOLET RADIATION.

All well-known British and Continental Spa Treatments administered on the most approved principles by fully qualified attendants, with accuracy and the utmost comfort. The charges are moderate.

TRAVEL SWIFTLY AND SMOOTHLY BY G.W.R.

TORQUAY MEDICAL BATHS

If you are interested, please write for complete informative literature to :
J. M. SCOTT, SPA DIRECTOR, TORQUAY.

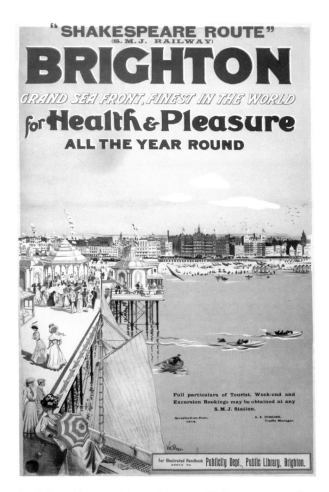

'Torquay for sunshine and spa treatments' advert, *The London Illustrated News*, July 1929.

'Brighton for Health & Pleasure all the year round' publicity poster, early twentieth century.

The Game of Good Health

PHARMACIES

Most companies manufacturing health products, as Glaxo and Wellcome, even if they had originated in small shops, seem to have preferred to operate on a wholesale basis rather than to develop a retailing arm. Exceptions were such firms as Boots and Allen & Hanburys. The latter had started, in 1715, as an apothecary shop, off Lombard Street in the City of London, run by Quaker Brothers – Silvanus and Timothy Bevan. In time, William Allen, who had been the Bevan's senior clerk, rose to take over the company, and it was he who introduced the Hanburys, linked to him by marriage. By 1856 the firm had become Allen & Hanburys, and it was the Hanburys and their descendants who came to run the business through to the 1950s.

Although the company was to grow to be a major manufacturer and wholesaler of pharmaceuticals and surgical equipment, it held on to its original City shop in Plough Court, through to its being bombed in WWII because 'it added much in prestige, historical continuity and advertisement to the brand Allen & Hanburys'. The firm also had an additional pharmacy, dispensing drugs, in Vere Street, near to the then expanding medical empire in Harley Street and adjacent roads. But the company was never to operate as a retailer outside London, except for some forays when trying to establish itself overseas. Even Vere Street was as much about compounding and wholesaling medicines as dispensing them to 'distinguished' customers. From Quaker origins the

Vitamin D in the 'Allenburys' Products

The following well-known 'Allenburys' Products have for some time been enriched by the addition of synthetic Vitamin D prepared by the new process of Ultra-Violet Light Irradiation.

The 'Allenburys'
Foods for Infants

The 'Allenburys'
Malted Rusks

The 'Allenburys' Diet

'Bynotone'

Amongst other notable advantages these products are therefore fully protective against rickets and allied disorders. *No change has been made in the packing or the directions for use.*

Allen & Hanburys Ltd.

Bethnal Green, London, E. 2.

Allenburys press advert, undated.

company was always about high quality and ethical products, but this, inevitably, meant higher prices and servicing the higher echelons of the market.

It was left to the likes of Timothy Whites and Boots to provide for the hoi polloi, Timothy White just pipping John Boot by one year when he opened his ship chandlers and general store in Portsmouth in 1848 (White did not actually qualify as a pharmacist until 1869). By the end of the century Timothy Whites had become one of a handful of chemists having more than a dozen shops throughout the country. Starting as it did as a general store, Timothy Whites was always to sell a wide range of goods beyond pharmaceuticals, and this balance was to continue when the firm merged with Taylors Drug Co. in 1935; by the time Boots took over Timothy Whites & Taylors in 1968 it had some 600 shops. After the takeover, Timothy Whites, although keeping its brand name, was reduced to selling just household goods, with Boots retaining the pharmaceutical side.

Although, for a period, Timothy White's was to be a major competitor of Boots, it was Boots which came to dominate the dispensing side of the pharmaceutical industry, with its own manufacturing plant and its own brands. John Boot had started out

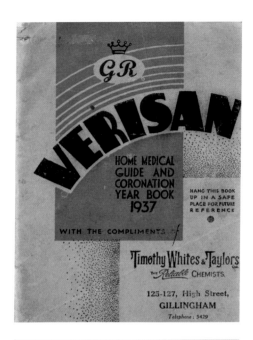

GR

VERISAN

HOME MEDICAL
GUIDE AND
CORONATION
YEAR BOOK
1937

HANG THIS BOOK
UP IN A SAFE
PLACE FOR FUTURE
REFERENCE

WITH THE COMPLIMENTS of

Timothy Whites & Taylors Ltd.
The *Reliable* CHEMISTS.

125-127, High Street,
GILLINGHAM
Telephone: 5429

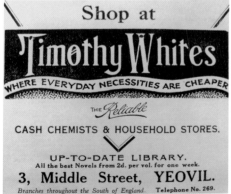

Shop at

Timothy Whites

WHERE EVERYDAY NECESSITIES ARE CHEAPER

THE *Reliable*

CASH CHEMISTS & HOUSEHOLD STORES.

UP-TO-DATE LIBRARY.
All the best Novels from 2d. per vol. for one week.

3, Middle Street, YEOVIL.
Branches throughout the South of England.   Telephone No. 269.

Visit

TIMOTHY WHITES

ABINGDON ST., BLACKPOOL

Large Selection of Gifts

Value and Variety

CHEMISTS
*Beauty Aids
and Cosmetics*

HOUSEWARES
*Everything for the
Home and Garden*

as a herbalist, opening his shop in Goose Gate in Nottingham in 1849. When he died, prematurely, in 1869, his young son Jesse, aged 10, helped his mother carry on at the shop, taking over full responsibility for the business in 1877. What must have been a rarity in large companies, it was only three Boots – John, Jesse, and his son John, who controlled the business until the mid-twentieth century.

In reverse order to Timothy Whites, Boots started with medicinal products but expanded rapidly into general and household goods, and services such as cafes and book lending. The Booklovers Library, at its height, was lending some thirty five million books a year. Jesse, unlike Allen & Hanburys, priced his prescriptions below that of other chemists, consequently attracting a wider customer base. Initially production of pharmaceuticals took place over the shop in Goose Gate, but with the expansion of the business, increasingly larger plants grew up on the outskirts of Nottingham, for quality control and the research of new products. Some early Boots own-lines were for throat pastilles and cold cream, with, later on, sun tan lotions and its cosmetic range – No.7. Ibuprofen, one of Boots' best known 'breakthroughs' did not come on to the market until the '60s.

Opposite right: Press advertisement for Timothy Whites, Blackpool, *c.*1950s. **Above:** Boots Chemists shop front, Muswell Hill, 1920.

It was Jesse who embarked on major advertising campaigns, initially just in the home locality, but gradually into the national press. By buying in bulk Jesse was able to adopt the tag 'Health for a Shilling'. In the 1930s Boots adopted the line that people should not just buy in emergencies but should stock up in advance. A campaign encouraging this was run around a cartoon family who with the 'Good Health Army' (Boots), fight the 'Bad Health Army', which included 'Brigadier Blood Poison, Flight Commander Influenza and Captain Sore Throat'. In addition to press advertisements there were children's games, a cartoon film, and more such, all featuring the family.

In the inter-war years Boots seem to have used a number of advertising agencies including Publicity Arts Ltd. and C. Vernon & Sons; and in the immediate post-war years, Everett's, Smith's, and Pritchard, Wood & Partners. It was Vernons who worked on the 'preventative' campaigns, with advertisements carrying copy suggesting 'the wise housewife keeps the essentials of home-doctoring and first-aid at hand in the bathroom cupboard'. With these, and others, James Fitton, the longtime art director of Vernons gave Boots a modernist image.

Above and right: 'See how they won' booklet, produced by Boots, undated.

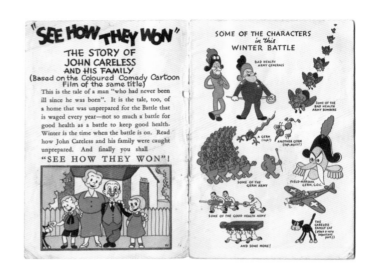

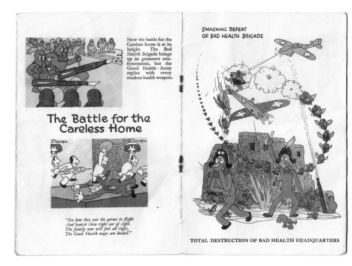

FROM OLIVE GROVE TO BOOTS THE CHEMISTS

CLEAR "virgin" Olive Oil, barrelled within sight of the picturesque groves, is shipped direct to Boots The Chemists—one of the largest importers of edible Olive Oil in Great Britain. Boots Olive Oil is transferred from barrels to bottles by special machinery under the most hygienic conditions. Every bottle is hermetically sealed and guaranteed full imperial measure. Direct handling of large quantities of Pure Olive Oil, from beginning to end, enables Boots The Chemists to guarantee absolute purity and perfect flavour at a reasonable price. Boots Olive Oil is best for salads, cookery and general household use.

Sold at the following reduced prices

1 pint bottle, 2/9   ½-pint bottle, 1/6   ¼-pint bottle, 10½d.

EVERY BOTTLE GUARANTEED FULL IMPERIAL MEASURE.

OVER 770 BRANCHES IN GREAT BRITAIN

O.O.8.   BOOTS PURE DRUG CO. LTD.

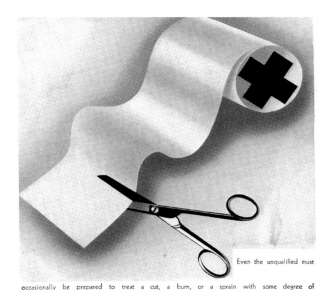

occasionally be prepared to treat a cut, a burn, or a sprain with some degree of ready skill. It is certainly a nuisance and it might be a tragedy if at every emergency we had to dash out to the chemists. The wise housewife keeps the essentials of home-doctoring and first-aid at hand in the bathroom cupboard. She can either buy a simple first-aid box or an economical stock of bandages, plaster, iodine, boric lint and antiseptic creams of all kinds at any of Boots 1080 branches.

FIRST FOR FIRST AID

Boots Pure Drug Co. Ltd., Nottingham.   cvp—6a

Left: 'From olive grove to Boots the chemists' press advert, 1926. **Above:** Boots press advertisement, 1937.

EPILOGUE

On reflection, when one considers the vast array of products and services related to health and safety, that were, and still are, available, for self-help, there must be an element of surprise to hear, nowadays, that A&E Departments are overwhelmed, hospitals short of beds and G.P.s overworked; the 'worried well' are still with us. Of course, since the 1960s, the end of the period covered by this book, vital statistics inform us of the increased proportion of the aged in the population, with all the ills that brings, the effects of ever growing pollution, the devious mutations of bacteria, a more sedentary life style and other such factors changing the nature of ailments. These have to be balanced against a general improvement in the standard of living, and a better educated awareness of health and safety issues, when assessing the overall state of the nation's health. Some diseases prevalent at the beginning of the twentieth century in Britain have been eradicated or greatly reduced, new ones have appeared; the medical sciences perpetually have to play catch up.

Whatever the situation, we are still, as we were, it would seem, susceptible to whatever is marketed as good for our health, particularly when claims are accompanied by images of handsome muscular men and lithesome sexy women, suggesting we could become like them if only we drank this, ate that, exercised in such and such a way, wore certain apparel, had our bathroom cabinets crammed and so on.

The paradox is that when more soundly grounded advice and interventions are made by government, they are viewed with suspicion, or seen as nannying interference. Governments only seem to move on health and safety matters when they are obliged to, and when they are reasonably sure of the soundness, in medical terms, of what they are offering; governments are conservative in this respect, tending to be more reactive than preventative. One has only to compare the anxiety that has surrounded government immunisation campaigns and our general disregard of sex education, with our enthusiasm for various commercially marketed health regimen, which, as fashion, change with the seasons. We seem only too willing to pop into the local health shop or to go online to seek an elixir for our ills. Plus ca change.

When one regards how health and safety cure-alls or cure-specifics have been marketed in the years covered by this book, its advertising does not appear to be able to claim any specific characteristics of its own compared to advertising in other fields. At the turn of the twentieth century its advertising tended to be earnest, adorned with floral ornamentation, with languid long-

'Drivers: Make sure you can always pull up within the range of your headlights', Tom Gentleman artwork for a poster for RoSPA, *c.*1940.

HERE'S TO YOUR HEALTH

tressed women, or mythological figures symbolic of strength or similar, much of this hanging on into the 1920s. But by then advertisers began to be more confident in using a lighter touch and humour entered the field, as with Bovril's pyjamed survivor, Eno's 'Can't and Can' family, Guinness' use of Gilroy and Bateman, and Beecham's employment of Bairnsfather.

Of course the style and content of advertising would differ as to whether a product or service was being launched, relaunched, coming out in a different form, or whether the advertiser merely needed to keep its name before the public, as in wartime. With health and safety advertising, although there are notable exceptions, early advertising relied more on copy-writers than on designers to explain in some detail the origins and benefits of what was on offer, with much use of endorsements from medical practitioners and celebrities, in this case more commonly from obviously healthy sportsmen and women than the stage and screen personalities used for beauty products.

As any product became successful the copy tended to be cut back, oft times to a mere catch phrase, and

'To keep fit inner cleanliness comes first', advert for Andrews liver salt, *Housewife*, January 1944.

the image simplified to just the product itself as with 'Good-night Bourn-vita', 'Drinka Pinta Milka Day' and 'Guinness is Good for You'.

From the 1930s onwards, photography began to be more frequently used, and by the post-war period had virtually replaced artwork. Crookes, for example, used half-page photographs of roaring seas to remind us of the origin of its halibut liver oil, and many products, as Dettol, used photographs of models playing doctors and patients, when conversations between the two were being portrayed. Sometimes photography and artwork would be combined, as with the photomontage of Henrion's VD posters. Nevertheless health and safety advertisers continued to make use of the great post-war commercial artists as Abram Games, Hans Schleger, Pat Keely, F.H.K. Henrion and Tom Eckersley, as their pre-war predecessors had commissioned the talented McKnight Kauffer and Ashley Havinden. Health & Safety advertising has had its share of iconic images, memorable tags, and remarkably successful campaigns, and can well serve as a genuine area of study for students interested in the history of advertising and its design in the twentieth century.

'Drinka Pinta Milka Day' poster, issued by the Milk Marketing Board, Patrick Tilley, 1959.

REFERENCES

1935 James McDonnell, *A Doctor Talks*, George Newnes.

1938 H.A. Clegg, *Brush up your Health*, J.M. Dent.

1969 comp. Peter Hadley, *The History of Bovril Advertising*, Ambassador Publishing Services.

1970 Norman Longmate, *Alive and Well, medicine and public health, 1830 to the present day*, Penguin.

1976 Peter Havins, *The Spas of England*, Robert Hale.

1980 Dr. Vernon Coleman, *The Home Pharmacy*, Pan.

1985 Brian Sibley, *The Book of Guiness Advertsing*.

1990 Geoffrey Tweedale, *At the Sign of the Plough: Allen & Hanburys and the British Pharmaceutical Industry, 1715–1990*, John Murray.

2001 Edgar Jones, *The Business of Medicine, the extraordinary history of Glaxo*, Profile Books.

2006 Timothy Wilcox, *A Day in the Sun*, Philip Wilson.

2007 Virginia Smith, *Clean, a history of personal hygiene and purity*, OUP.

2008 Peter Homan et al, *Popular Medicines: an illustrated history*, Pharmaceutical Press.

2008 David Newton, *Trademarked*, Sutton Publishing.

2009 *A history of Boots*, Boots Archive.

2011 Charlotte Macdonald, *Strong, Beautiful and Modern: national fitness in Britain, New Zealand and Canada, 1935–1960*, UBC Press.

2012 Scott Anthony, *Public Relations and the Making of Modern Britain*, Manchester University Press.

2014 Ruth Artmonsky, *Moving the Hearts and Minds of Men, Bill Crawford, ad man*, Artmonsky Arts.

2014 David Eves, *Two steps forward, one step back*, available online.

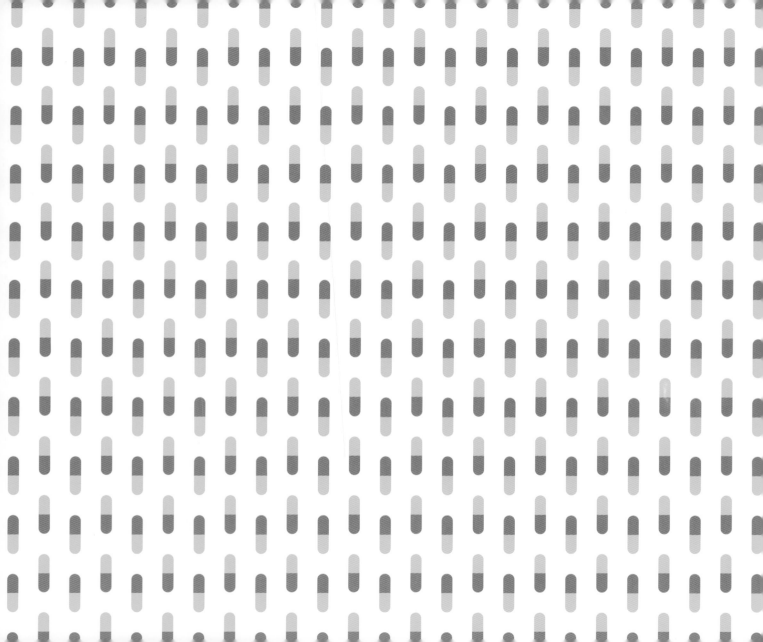